Walk Around

TBF/TBM Avenger

By Lou Drendel

Color by Lou Drendel, Don Greer, and Richard Hudson

Illustrated by Ernesto Cumpian and Andrew Probert

Walk Around Number 25

squadron/signal publications

Introduction

The **TBF/TBM Avenger** was among the class of modern combat aircraft designed and built for the US Navy in the early 1940s. It was the most prolific torpedo bomber of World War II, with a total of 9,839 built by Grumman and General Motors between 1940 and 1945. The Avenger served with the US Navy, US Marines, Britain's Royal Navy, and the Royal New Zealand Air Force during the war. This aircraft wasn't just prolific; it was pre-eminent.

The Avenger grew out of a 1939 US Navy Bureau of Aeronautics (BuAer) specification, which called for a new torpedo bomber capable of 300 mph (482.8 кмн). This also called for internal carriage of three 500 pound (226.8 кg) bombs or one torpedo and a 3000 mile (4827.9 км) scouting range with a bomb bay-mounted auxiliary fuel tank. Defensive armament was specified as a pair of forward-firing machine guns, a power turret, and hand-held ventral guns.

Two companies competed for the contract. Vought's entry was the **XTBU-1 Sea Wolf**, while Grumman designed the XTBF-1 Avenger. This was Grumman's first torpedo bomber, but its design clearly shows the F4F Wildcat fighter lineage. The XTBF-1 featured the first electric powered turret ever installed on an aircraft. (All previous power turrets were either mechanical or hydraulic.) The Navy ordered two prototypes of each design on 8 April 1940. The TBU and TBF were closely matched in many respects; however, the TBF was lighter, faster, and – most important from the Navy's standpoint – could reduce its wingspan from 54 feet 2 inches (16.5 м) to 19 feet (5.8 м) when the wings were folded. The Navy ordered 286 TBF-1s from Grumman in December of 1940.

The first XTBF-1 made its maiden flight on 7 August 1941. The new aircraft was named the Avenger after the Japanese attack on Pearl Harbor on 7 December 1941, which brought the US into World War II. The first production TBF was delivered in January of 1942 and Grumman was producing 60 Avengers per month by June of that year. Production exceeded 100 aircraft per month by November and averaged 150 per month in 1943, which was the last year Grumman produced the TBF. Since Grumman was now concentrating on producing the F6F Hellcat fighter, the US Navy Department awarded a production contract for the Avenger to the Eastern Aircraft Division of General Motors. Eastern Aircraft's version of the Avenger – designated the TBM – began production in 1942. The TBM was produced in over three times the numbers of the TBF before the line was shut down in September of 1945.

The Avenger's combat debut at the Battle of Midway was not auspicious. Six TBF-1s of Torpedo Squadron 8 took off from Midway on the morning of 4 June 1942 to attack the approaching Japanese fleet. Only one of the six TBF-1s survived the attack and it crash-landed back on Midway with the turret gunner dead and both the pilot and radioman wounded. The unsuccessful attacks by the six Avengers and other Midway-based aircraft did succeed in delaying the Japanese follow-up attack on the island. The decks of the Japanese carriers were full of bomb-laden aircraft when dive bombers from the USS ENTERPRISE (CV-6) and USS YORKTOWN (CV-5) found and attacked the enemy warships. All four Japanese carriers were sunk in what became the pivotal battle of the Pacific war.

The Avenger was the only torpedo bomber flown by US forces in combat after 1942. It replaced the obsolete Douglas **TBD Devastator**, which had been severely mauled in combat. The TBF/TBM played a major role in the march across the Pacific and was also one of the most important instruments in winning the submarine war in the Atlantic.

The Avenger was initially used primarily as a glide bomber because US aerial torpedoes performed poorly. The TBF/TBM had a maximum ordnance load of 2000 pounds. (907.2 кg), which comprised a mix of bombs, rockets, and depth charges. Torpedoes were largely abandoned after Midway and were not carried regularly again until after June of 1944, when improvements mandated their use once again. By that time, it was rare for American aircraft to encounter enemy shipping at sea and the Avenger was primarily employed as a ground support weapon in the march across the Pacific. In the Atlantic, Avengers employing depth charges and bombs played a pivotal role in the defeat and destruction of the German U-boat (submarine) menace to Allied shipping.

The post-war development of the Avenger included a more sophisticated Anti-Submarine Warfare (ASW) version for the U.S. Navy. The TBM-3W was equipped with a large ventral radome, while the TBM-3S filled the ASW strike role, and the TBM-3Q was used for radar counter-measures. Additional versions included the TBM-3N night attacker, the TBM-3U utility aircraft, and the TBM-3R transport. Avengers served with the US Navy until 1954.

Surplus TBMs were delivered after World War II to Canada, France, the United Kingdom, Japan, the Netherlands, Uruguay, and Brazil. Even after all Avengers were phased out of military service, they continued to serve as aerial fire fighters for the US Forestry Service. Several Avengers survive today as restored warbirds and they are regularly flown in air shows in the United States.

Acknowledgements

In addition to the official sources of Grumman, US Navy, and the USMC, the efforts of several private collectors and photographers made this book possible. As always, my longtime friend and tireless contributor, Norm Taylor, played a major role. I am also grateful to Warren Bodie, Ted Carlson, Walt Houghton, Ed Deigan, Steve Kraus, Clyde Gerdes, and Glen Phillips for their contributions.

COPYRIGHT 2001 SQUADRON/SIGNAL PUBLICATIONS, INC.
1115 CROWLEY DRIVE CARROLLTON, TEXAS 75011-5010

All rights reserved. No part of this publication may be reproduced, stored in a retrieval system or transmitted in any form by means electrical, mechanical or otherwise, without written permission of the publisher.

ISBN 0-89747-424-4

If you have any photographs of aircraft, armor, soldiers or ships of any nation, particularly wartime snapshots, why not share them with us and help make Squadron/Signal's books all the more interesting and complete in the future. Any photograph sent to us will be copied and the original returned. The donor will be fully credited for any photos used. Please send them to:

**Squadron/Signal Publications, Inc.
1115 Crowley Drive
Carrollton, TX 75011-5010**

Если у вас есть фотографии самолётов, вооружения, солдат или кораблей любой страны, особенно, снимки времён войны, поделитесь с нами и помогите сделать новые книги издательства Эскадрон/Сигнал ещё интереснее. Мы переснимем ваши фотографии и вернём оригиналы. Имена приславших снимки будут сопровождать все опубликованные фотографии. Пожалуйста, присылайте фотографии по адресу:

**Squadron/Signal Publications, Inc.
1115 Crowley Drive
Carrollton, TX 75011-5010**

軍用機、装甲車両、兵士、軍艦などの写真を所持しておられる方はいらっしゃいませんか？どの国のものでも結構です。作戦中に撮影されたものが特に良いのです。Squadron/Signal 社の出版する刊行物において、このような写真は内容を一層充実し、興味深いものとすることができます。当方にお送り頂いた写真は、複写の後お返しいたします。出版物中に写真を使用した場合は、必ず提供者のお名前を明記させて頂きます。お写真は下記にご送付ください。

**Squadron/Signal Publications, Inc.
1115 Crowley Drive
Carrollton, TX 75011-5010**

(Front Cover) This TBM-3 Avenger, Black 66, was assigned to Night Torpedo Squadron 90 (VT(N)-90) aboard the aircraft carrier USS ENTERPRISE (CV-6) in March of 1945. ENTERPRISE's Avengers flew night intruder missions and were fitted with exhaust flame dampers to hide the flames from enemy eyes. The TBM's undersurfaces were painted Flat Black for these missions.

(Previous Page) An early TBF-1 Avenger is airborne on a Grumman factory acceptance flight in 1942. The cowl-mounted .30 caliber (7.62мм) machine gun would be replaced with two wing mounted .50 caliber (12.7мм) machine guns in the TBF-1C, which entered production on 12 July 1943. (Grumman)

(Back Cover) The three-man crew of TBM-3 Black 3 discuss attack profiles against German U-boats (submarines) on the deck of their escort carrier (CVE) in the Atlantic in 1944. This aircraft's wings were folded back to allow for easier storage aboard the confines of an aircraft carrier.

The first production Avenger was this TBF-1 (BuNo 00373), sitting on the Grumman ramp at Bethpage, New York on 9 January 1942. The lowered flaps were hydraulically operated, as were the landing gear and bomb bay doors. Production TBF-1s differed from the XTBF-1 prototype in having the engine moved 11 inches (27.9 CM) forward and the tail surfaces enlarged. These measures corrected the XTBF-1's center of gravity (CG) and directional stability problems. (Grumman)

This early production TBF-1 was fitted with the cuffed Curtiss Electric propeller used by Grumman's F4F Wildcat fighter. The unique wing fold mechanism common to many Grumman aircraft was invented by company founder Leroy Grumman using a paper clip stuck in an eraser. This mechanism reduced the Avenger's wing span to 19 feet (5.8 M) without increasing the aircraft's height. (Grumman)

The TBF-1 had a wingspan of 54 feet 2 inches (16.5 M); this wingspan remained the same for all subsequent Avengers. Fixed slots placed in the outboard wing leading edges guided air over the ailerons at high angles of attack. These slots – used in all Avenger models – prevented the aircraft from stalling. The total cost of the two XTBF-1 prototypes, including plans and ground testing, was only $556,000. (Grumman)

The rear view of the Avenger remained essentially unchanged throughout all versions, beginning with the first production TBF-1. The single .50 caliber (12.7MM) turret mounted Colt-Browning M2 machine gun was offset to the right of the aircraft's centerline. US Navy aircraft displayed the national insignia on the upper left and lower right wing surfaces from 26 February 1941 until 5 January 1942. (Grumman)

(Above Left) This restored TBM-3 Avenger (White 88) starts its 1900 horsepower (HP) Wright R-2600-20 Cyclone engine at the Experimental Aircraft Association (EAA) Fly-In at Oshkosh, Wisconsin in 1997. The Avenger was painted in the three-tone camouflage scheme of Sea Blue on the uppersurfaces, Intermediate Blue (FS35164) on the sides, and Non-Specular (NS) White (FS37855) on the undersurfaces. The Sea Blue was NS, or flat (FS35042) on the upper fuselage and the leading edges of the wings and horizontal stabilizers. The rest of the wing and horizontal stabilizer upper surfaces were Semi-Gloss Sea Blue (FS25042). The white inverted arrowhead on White 88's rudder was the insignia of the escort carrier USS NEHENTA BAY (CVE-74), which operated in the Pacific in 1944 and 1945. An unknown insignia appeared on the TBM's nose. (Lou Drendel)

(Above) Coke Stuart restored this TBM-3 (NL7001C/BuNo 85794) in the markings of the TBM-1C flown by Lt (JG) George Bush – the future 41st President of the United States. Bush was assigned to VT-51 aboard the light carrier USS SAN JACINTO (CVL-30) in 1944. On 2 September 1944, Bush's Avenger was shot down by Japanese anti-aircraft fire over Chichi Jima in the Bonin Islands. His turret gunner and radio operator were killed and Bush bailed out of the aircraft into the coastal water, where he was picked up by the submarine USS FINBACK (SS-230). Stuart's restored TBM-3 flew in 22 combat missions from the USS YORKTOWN (CV-10) in 1945. (Walt Houghton)

(Left) This well restored TBM-3 (Black 25) was displayed at Elkhart, Indiana on 5 June 1998. The Avenger was finished in the Atlantic Anti-Submarine Scheme II, which consisted of Dark Gull Gray (FS36231) uppersurfaces and NS White (FS37855) sides and undersurfaces. The inner surfaces of the landing gear doors, gear bays, and wing fold mechanism were also painted NS White. The Insignia of Composite Squadron 13 (VC-13) was painted on the TBM's nose. The 14 German flags in four rows under the cockpit indicated 'kills' against German U-boats and surface vessels. (Lou Drendel)

Two restored TBM-3E Avengers fly in close formation off of Ft. Lauderdale, Florida prior to making a fly by of the carrier USS AMERICA (CV-66). The near TBM was finished in overall Glossy Sea Blue (FS15042), while the far aircraft has Glossy Sea Blue uppersurfaces and White undersurfaces – an unauthentic color scheme. The near Avenger was also fitted with a modern radio antenna on the aft canopy just ahead of the turret. The Avenger is a popular aircraft on the warbird circuit, due to its handling and performance. The TBF/TBM's relatively economical operating costs are well appreciated by their owners. (Walt Houghton)

This TBM-3 (Yellow 54) is part of the collection of the Cavanaugh Flight Museum in Addison, Texas, a Dallas suburb. The Avenger was finished in overall Glossy Sea Blue with a white tail band and two yellow aft fuselage stripes. The tail and aft fuselage markings identified an aircraft assigned to the escort carrier USS CAPE GLOUCESTER (CVE-109) in 1945. This carrier embarked Marine Carrier Air Group 4 (MCVG-4), which included the TBMs of Marine Torpedo Bomber Squadron 132 (VMTB-132). The CAPE GLOUCESTER saw action off the Japanese coast from July of 1945 until Japan's surrender on 14 August 1945. (Glen Phillips)

(Right) This well-restored TBM-3R (N452HA) taxies at Lakeland, Florida during the 1999 EAA Sun n' Fun fly in. The -3R version was used as a Carrier On-Board (COD) delivery aircraft during the Korean War. The turret and all armament were removed and the canopy extended to the leading edge of the dorsal fin. The TBM-3R could carry seven passengers or various cargo items between shore bases and the aircraft carrier. This Avenger appeared in a non-standard finish of Glossy Sea Blue over Intermediate Blue, with no Insignia Red on the national insignia. An Instrument Landing System (ILS) blade antenna was added to the aircraft's vertical stabilizer, just ahead of the rudder hinge. The Avenger has proven to be a popular warbird: stable, easy to fly, and reliable. Over 100 Avengers survive worldwide. (Lou Drendel)

A primary identifying characteristic of the TBF-1 was the shortened cowl flaps. The aircraft was fitted with the cowl flap on the upper cowling surfaces to allow heat to escape from the engine area. The oil cooler air flap was mounted aft of the cowling and ahead of the wing leading edge. These flaps were usually open when the aircraft was warming up its engine. This early Avenger was armed and had the additional glass fairing forward of the turret. This glass fairing was deleted from the TBF-1C and later Avenger models. The 13 stripes on the rudder – seven red, six white – were required on US Navy aircraft from 23 December 1941 until 6 May 1942. The stripes and the red portions of the national insignia were deleted on 6 May, to prevent US aircraft from being confused with Japanese aircraft, which used the red *Hinomaru* (rising sun) insignia. (Grumman)

General Arrangement

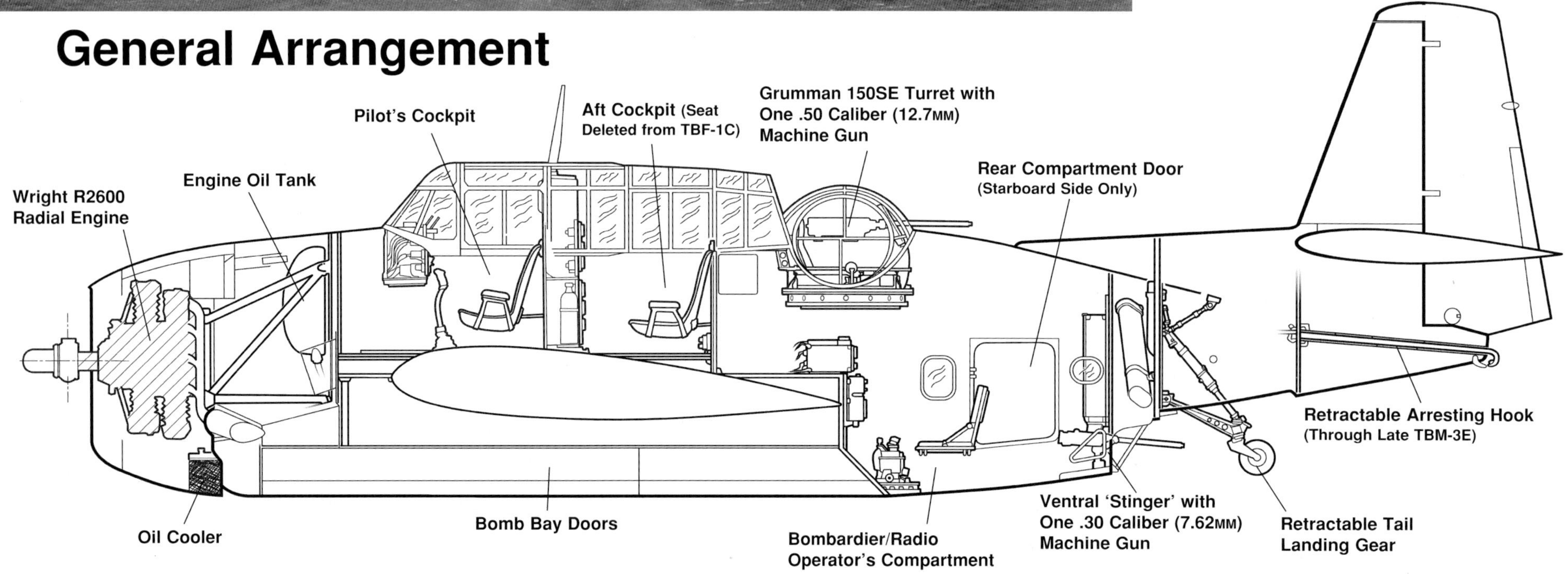

The 11th production TBF-1 Avenger (BuNo 00383) was parked at Grumman's Bethpage, Long Island, New York factory prior to acceptance by the US Navy in 1942. The aircraft is finished in Non-Specular (NS) Blue-Gray (FS35189) over NS Light Gray (FS36440), with the national insignia applied to the fuselage and both the left and right wing upper and lower surfaces. The vertical antenna placed beside the wing national insignia is the TBF-1's starboard Yagi antenna. This antenna, with an identical unit mounted under the port wing, provided transmission and reception for the aircraft's Westinghouse Air-to-Surface Type B (ASB) radar. The radar provided information on the location of surface targets to the Avenger's bombardier at night and under all weather conditions. (Grumman)

A TBF-1 (22-C-8, BuNo 55051) flies low over the water on a practice mission during the first half of 1943. This Avenger was assigned to Composite Squadron 22 (VC-22) aboard the light carrier USS INDEPENDENCE (CVL-22). The three-tone color scheme of Sea Blue, Intermediate Blue, and White was applied to this aircraft, which has black fuselage codes. These codes were usually reduced to the individual aircraft numbers when the Squadron entered the combat zone, to deny unit information to enemy intelligence. The Grumman 150SE rear turret was turned fully to the starboard beam firing position. The TBF-1 was distinguished from later Avenger models by the nose-mounted .30 caliber (7.62MM) Colt-Browning M2 machine gun, its short cowl flaps, and the open oil cooler door just ahead of the wing root. (US Navy via Warren Bodie)

The wings were folded back on this restored TBM-3, which participated in the EAA Fly-In at Oshkosh in 1997. The TBM-3 series was identified by air intakes located at the top and bottom of the cowl; the earlier TBF/TBM-1 only had the upper cowl intake. The later model's full-surround cowl flaps provided additional air cooling of the more powerful 1900 hp Wright R-2600-20 radial engine. (Lou Drendel)

All Avenger models were fitted with the three-bladed, all-metal Hamilton Standard Hydromatic propeller, which measured 13 feet 1 inch (4 m) in diameter. The pilot could hydraulically adjust the propeller pitch from 22° to 49° for improved engine efficiency. The propeller reduction gearbox was placed behind the hub and the propeller governor was mounted on top of this gearbox. (Lou Drendel)

The bulge on the TBM-3's lower front cowling accommodated the oil cooler intake. The tube protruding from the lower cowl was the oil overflow pan drain, from which excess engine oil was vented from the aircraft. This restored Avenger's cowling was marked BOUNCING BELCH BEER HAULER GUADALCANAL 1943. (Lou Drendel)

This Avenger – and all other production examples – was equipped with the Hamilton Standard constant speed propeller, while the two Avenger prototypes used Curtiss Electric propellers. The spinner dome was filled with engine oil to operate the propeller pitch mechanism. The TBM-3's R-2600-20 engines had 14 cylinders in two rows. This TBM-3's propeller blades and spinner dome were painted black, while the hub was left in natural metal. (Lou Drendel)

Deployed aboard a carrier during 1942, this TBF-1 has this model's standard cooler intake, fitted to the upper cowling. The Avenger's first combat was at the Battle of Midway on 4 June 1942, when six land-based TBF-1s of VT-8 attacked the Japanese fleet. Japanese fighters shot down five of the six Avengers and the only survivor crash-landed on Midway with the turret gunner killed and both the pilot and bombardier/ventral gunner wounded. (US Navy via Warren Bodie)

The nose of this TBM-3 differed from the earlier TBF-1 in adding a lower cooler intake, which was slightly wider than the upper intake. The upper cooler intake also fed air into the R-2600-20 engine's twin carburetors, which sent air and fuel into the engine cylinders for combustion. The silver ring around the propeller reduction gearbox housed the ignition wires. These wires were connected to a spark plug fitted to each of the engine's 14 cylinders. (Lou Drendel)

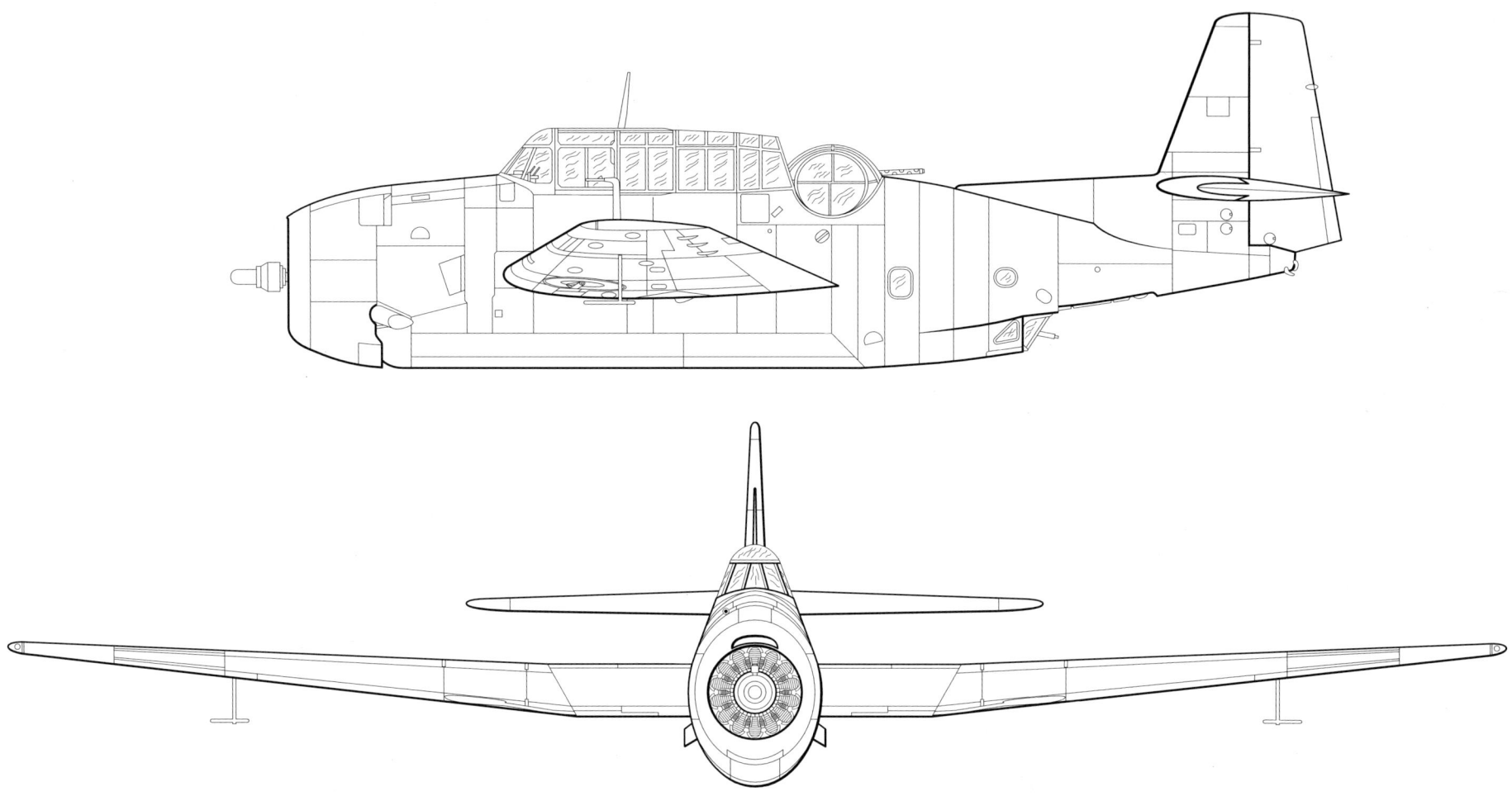

Grumman/Eastern Aircraft TBF-1/TBM-1 Avenger Specifications

Wingspan.....................54 feet 2 inches (16.5 M)
Length..........................40 feet (12.2 M)
Height ....16 feet 5 inches (5 M)
Empty Weight..............10,080 pounds (4572.3 KG)
Maximum Weight........13,667 pounds (6199.4 KG)
Powerplant...................One 1700 HP Wright R-2600-8 Cyclone 14-cylinder, air-cooled, radial engine
Defensive Armament..One cowl-mounted .30 caliber (7.62MM) Colt-Browning M2 machine gun with 300 rounds; one turret-mounted .50 caliber (12.7MM) Colt-Browning M2 machine gun with 400 rounds, and one ventral-mounted .30 caliber Colt-Browning M2 machine gun with 500 rounds.

Offensive Armament.....One 22.4 inch (56.9 CM) Bliss-Leavitt Mark 13 torpedo or maximum of 2000 pounds (907.2 KG) of bombs or depth charges in bomb bay.
Maximum Speed............271 MPH (436.1 KMH) at 12,000 feet (3657.6 M)
Service Ceiling ....22,400 feet (6827.5 M)
Maximum Range...........1215 miles (1955.3 KM) with torpedo; 1450 miles (2333.5 KM) as scout
Crew..............................Three

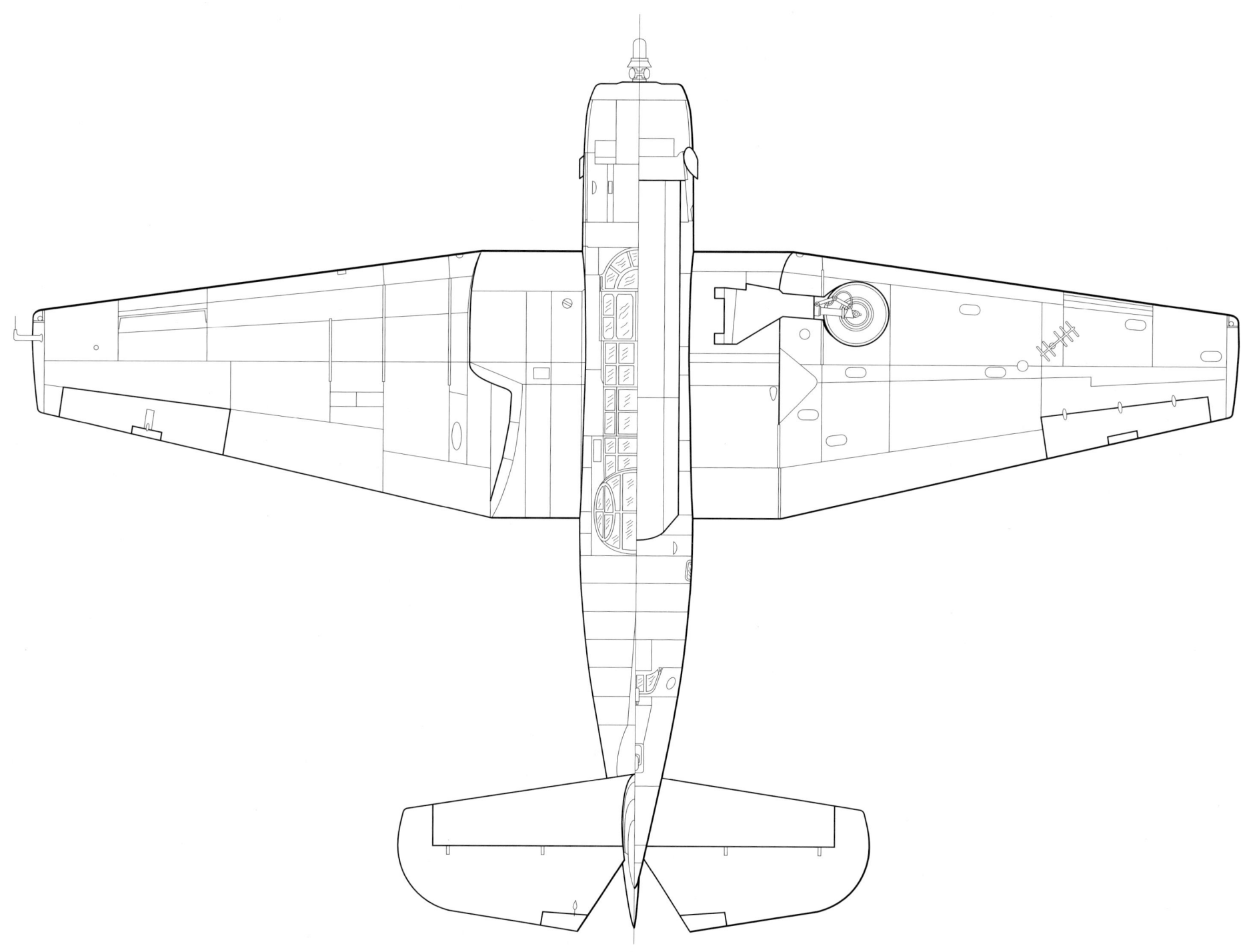

The engine oil tank was placed immediately in front of the engine compartment bulkhead, flanked to port and starboard by the engine mounting struts. Oil was placed into the tank through the filler vent at the upper left side of the oil tank, which was covered by a yellow cap. Holes along the panel's sides held flush-fitting screws used to secure the access panel. (Lou Drendel)

The TBM-3's cowl flaps were opened to reveal the engine exhaust collector ring. Exhaust from the engine's 14 cylinders was collected by this ring and vented out of the aircraft through either the port or starboard exhaust pipe. Three rods activated each set of cowl flaps, extending the flaps to release more hot air from the engine or retracting them when engine temperatures were normal. (Lou Drendel)

The port cowl access panel was removed to reveal the engine mount struts fitted to the TBM-3's engine compartment bulkhead. The engine oil tank beside the engine mount had a total capacity of 32 gallons (121.1 L); however, the TBM's normal oil load was 13 gallons (49.2 L). The thin, temporarily disconnected fore-aft rods beside the engine mounts connected the propeller pitch control in the cockpit with the pitch mechanism in the engine's front. The nose art on this restored TBM played on the Avenger's nickname, the 'turkey.' (Lou Drendel)

The port exhaust stack on the TBM-3 vented out exhaust gases from the seven left cylinders of the R-2600-20 engine. The starboard exhaust stack – through which fumes from the seven right cylinders were removed from the aircraft – was identical in appearance. Hot exhaust gases darkened the metal exhaust stack after only a short period of use. The base of the exhaust stack was fastened to the exhaust collector ring – which brought the exhaust gases from the engine's cylinders – by a clamp with two bolts. (Lou Drendel)

The cowl flaps were extended on this idle TBM-3's engine cowling. The cowl flaps were fully opened during engine warm up and ground operation and partially open for climbing to cruise altitude. These flaps were usually closed for level flight and cruising climbs under normal temperature conditions. The oil overflow pan drain was placed on the lower port cowling area. (Lou Drendel)

Cowl flap actuating rods adjusted the position of these flaps based on input from the cockpit. The pilot could set the cowl flaps in either the open, closed, or neutral (intermediate) positions. The earlier TBF/TBM-1 had only one cowl flap per cowling side, as opposed to the TBM-3's four flaps per side. The exhaust collector ring fed engine exhausts to the exhaust stack. (Lou Drendel)

A TBF-1C is prepared for launching from an aircraft carrier in mid-1944. A cable bridle from the catapult shuttle was fitted to hooks fixed to the Avenger's port and starboard main landing gear door to pull the aircraft with the shuttle. The bridle dropped off the aircraft into the sea after the aircraft was launched. This Avenger was armed with a .50 caliber (12.7mm) machine gun in each wing and was fitted with four 70 inch (177.8 cm) Mark 4 rocket launch rails under each wing. The upper cowling flap and the lower oil cooler flap were opened for the TBF's launch. An AN-N6 gun camera is fitted ahead of the windshield to record the results of the TBF-1C's gun firing. (Associated Press from US Navy)

US Marine ground crews prepare a TBM-3 for a mission from Tientsin (now Tianjin), China in the fall of 1945. Ground crewmen pulled the propeller blades through at least four revolutions to move oil into the cylinders prior to starting the engine. A discarded R-2600 engine was placed in front of the aircraft's starboard wing. This Avenger was equipped with four pairs of Mark 5 zero length rocket launch mounts under each wing. The bomb bay doors were open prior to being loaded with ordnance for the mission. US Marines were sent to China in October of 1945 to accept the surrender of Japanese forces there and to help keep order in chaotic post-war China. (Norman E. Taylor Collection)

(Above Left) Late model TBM-3s were delivered without the Mark 11 ring and post gunsight, which was fitted to previous Avenger models. The Mark 11 served as a manual back-up to the Mark 8 reflector gunsight installed aboard the aircraft. This particular restoration also lacks the Mark 8, which was the pilot's primary aiming device for the forward machine guns. An AN-N6 gun camera was placed in front of the windshield; TBF/TBM Avengers did not often carry this item. This restored TBM-3 was painted in an inaccurate camouflage scheme, with the area under the cowl flaps in polished metal instead of being painted to match the fuselage camouflage. Three Japanese 'rising sun' flags and two torpedoes were painted under the windshield, while the pilot's port and starboard canopy sections were slid back to the open position. (Lou Drendel)

(Above) The cowl flaps were fully opened on this restored TBM-3 on display. The AN-A6 gun camera is mounted on top of the nose, aft of the cowling. The post of the Mark 11 ring and post sight is positioned behind the gun camera. The pilot lined up the bead on top of the post with the crosshairs of the ring directly behind the post to aim his machine guns at the target. The more advanced reflector gunsight – in which the aiming point was projected onto an angled glass screen for the pilot – provided the lead angle for a swiftly moving target. The Mark 8 and other reflector sights superceded the ring and post gunsight during World War II. (Lou Drendel)

(Left) The TBF/TBM's AN-N6 gun camera was mounted on a platform slightly above the aircraft's upper surface and was controlled through a cable attached to the camera's starboard side. It was a 35MM fixed focus type, equipped with a film footage indicator and a film speed adjusting knob, which operated any time the aircraft's guns were fired. Intelligence personnel used gun camera footage to confirm air-to-air victory claims and to evaluate air combat tactics. (Lou Drendel)

A restored TBM-3E flies over Chino, California on 17 May 1987. Late production TBM-3Es – beginning with BuNo 86175 – replaced the fully retractable tail hook of earlier Avengers with a non-retractable external tail hook. The ventral machine gun position was deleted and the cowl flaps were of equal size, with the bottom two flaps lacking the indentation found with earlier TBMs. The pilot of this aircraft partially opened his port and starboard sliding canopy hoods, which allowed fresh air into the cockpit. Many Avenger pilots – particularly those who flew TBD Devastators before and early in World War II – preferred to fly with the canopy open as much as possible. The canopy was opened for both launch and recovery to ease an emergency exit from the aircraft in the event of an accident. (Ted Carlson/Fotodynamics)

Flight Compartment Windows

All TBF/TBM windows made from Plexiglas.

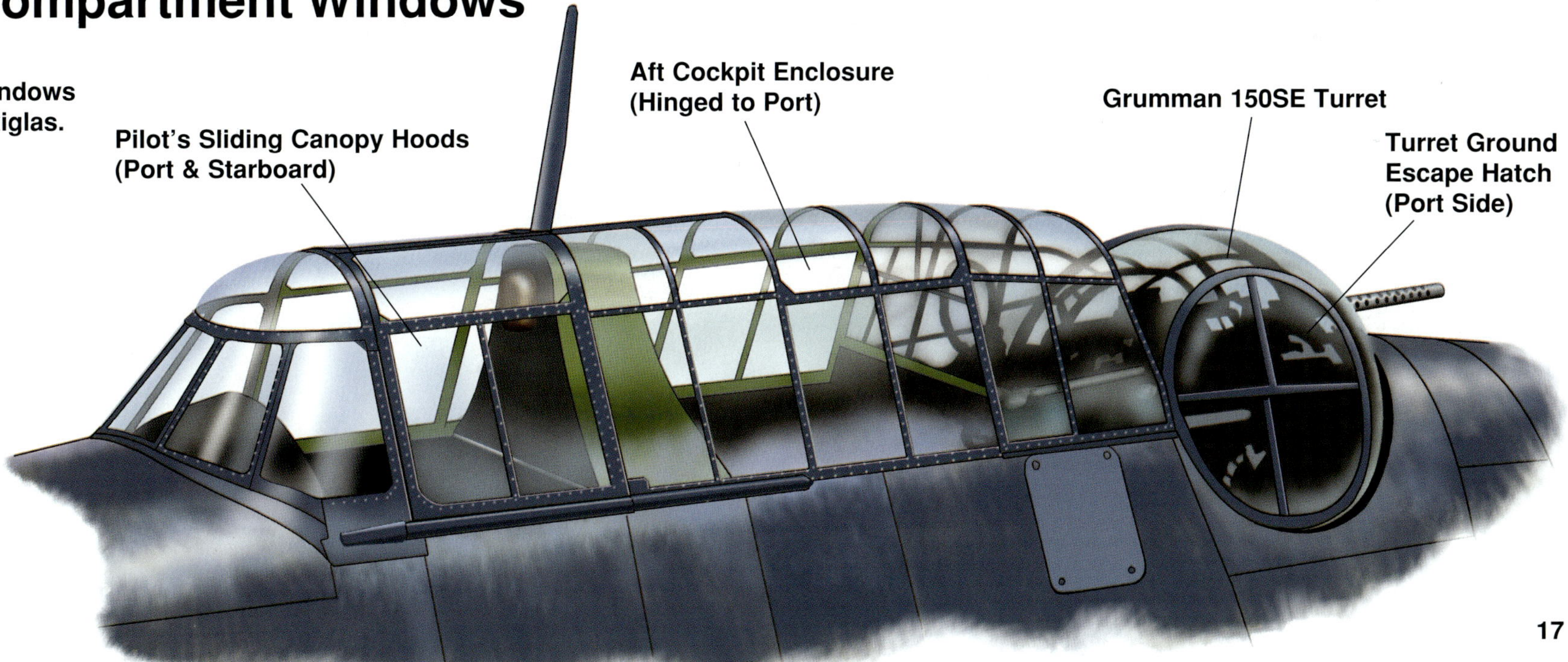

Pilot's Sliding Canopy Hoods (Port & Starboard)

Aft Cockpit Enclosure (Hinged to Port)

Grumman 150SE Turret

Turret Ground Escape Hatch (Port Side)

The TBF-1's instrument panel was topped by a padded leather-covered coaming. The top row of instruments consisted of (L-R): direction indicator, altimeter, directional gyro, and artificial horizon. The instruments arrayed below were: manifold pressure gage, tachometer, air speed indicator, turn and bank indicator, and rate of climb indicator. The pull out plotting board used for navigation was located just under the instrument panel. The control stick was pulled to starboard, which allowed a clear view of the main instrument panel. The remote indicating compass was installed atop the center console, immediately ahead of the control stick's neutral position. (Grumman)

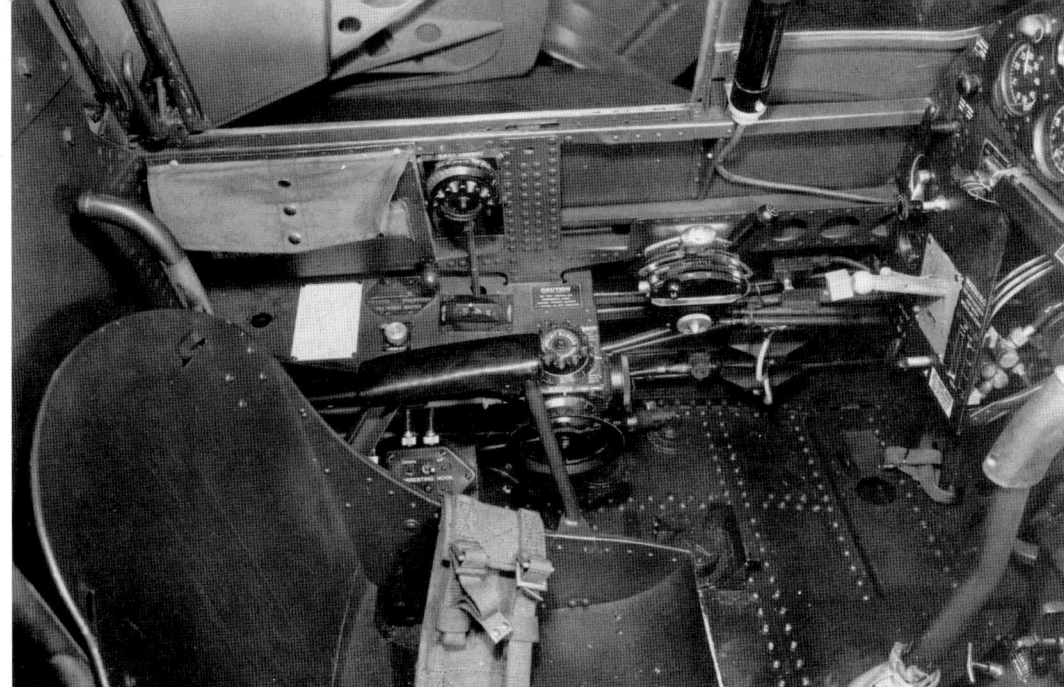

The flap and landing gear control levers were placed on the TBF-1's port instrument panel section. The throttle quadrant was placed aft of this panel under the canopy rail. The supercharger control was mounted outboard of the throttle. Rudder and elevator trim controls were behind the throttle quadrant, while the arresting gear (tail hook) control switch was located beside the pilot's seat edge. (Grumman)

The electrical distribution panel was located immediately aft of the starboard instrument panel section. Radio controls were placed above and below the right side console. Above the seat armrest was the signal flare launcher, with racks for flares aft of this launcher. The pilot's seat had room to allow a parachute to be worn as a seat cushion. (Grumman)

The TBM-3's seatback armor plate and padded headrest were the same in earlier Avenger models. The armor plate behind the pilot's seat was .375 inch (9.5MM) thick, while the armor supporting the headrest was .75 inch (19.1MM) thick. The TBM-3 pilot's seat height was adjusted using steel springs behind the seat, which replaced shock cords fitted to earlier Avenger models. (Lou Drendel)

A Mark 8 reflector gunsight was mounted atop the instrument panel shroud under the TBM-3's windshield. This sight allowed pilots to line up aerial targets for the two wing-mounted .50 caliber (12.7MM) machine guns and for torpedo attacks. A magnetic compass was placed under the windshield's uppermost panel to allow accurate readings without undue interference by the aircraft's metal structure. (Lou Drendel)

The pilot's canopy on all Avengers was split port and starboard. Either side canopy panel moved independently along the canopy center support. The panels were either locked closed, opened, or in one of three intermediate positions. Tan rubber seals were placed along the center support sides. These seals prevented water from falling into the cockpit through gaps in the canopy panels. (Lou Drendel)

This restored TBM-3 included a seat cushion for the pilot and modern nylon seat belts. Pilots of wartime Avengers used their parachutes as seat cushions, while seat belts were canvas with metal buckles and fittings. Arm rests fitted to the seat reduced pilot fatigue on long missions – as long as 13 hours in the case of the 'Night Owl' dusk-to-dawn anti-submarine patrols mounted in the Atlantic from 1944 to 1945. The pilot's manual referenced the heavy control forces required for maneuvering the Avenger. The control forces prohibited aileron rolls, snap rolls, Immelmann turns, inverted flight, and intentional spins. These were many restrictions for a single engine combat aircraft! (Lou Drendel)

The TBM's landing gear and flap controls were placed in the lower left corner of the instrument panel. The long lever with a red square knob activated the landing gear, while the shorter lever with the black round knob operated the flaps. Some Avengers had the flaps and landing gear interconnected. The hydraulically operated landing gear took 15 seconds to retract and 12 seconds to extend. Modern navigation instruments were placed in this aircraft's starboard instrument panel. (Lou Drendel)

Modern avionics were placed in a radio stack immediately beneath the throttle quadrant of the Cavanaugh Flight Museum's TBM-3 Avenger. These avionics and the modern seat belts and cushion are the only items out of place in a wartime Avenger cockpit. The mixture lever for regulating the amount of fuel and air entering the engine was mounted inboard of the throttle. The basic interior color on Eastern-made TBMs was Interior Green (FS34151), while Grumman-built TBFs used Bronze Green (FS34058). The red item on the front of the control stick grip covered the trigger for the Avenger's two wing-mounted .50 caliber (12.7mm) machine guns. The red bottom on top of the grip was the pilot's radio 'talk' button, pressed when speaking into his throat-mounted microphone. (Lou Drendel)

The TBM's center console controlled fuel flow from the aircraft's three main fuel tanks. The fuel tanks – under the cockpit and inside the inner wing sections – held 325 gallons (1230.3 L) of 100-octane gasoline. The three switches with red guards activated the fuel pumps and the larger red lever above selected the fuel tank to be used. The small panel on top of this console was a modern intercom system retrofitted to Cavanaugh's Avenger. The two rudder pedals flanked the center console on the cockpit floor. (Lou Drendel)

Several modern instruments were installed in the upper right instrument panel of the Cavanaugh Flight Museum's Avenger. Controls under the plotting board included the yellow cowl flap crank (port) and the red wing fold crank (starboard). The bomb bay door control was placed in the lower panel's center. (Lou Drendel)

The flap and landing gear handles were placed on the TBM instrument panel's port side. The flap lever had a red square handle, while the landing gear lever used a black round handle. The size and shape of these handles allowed for easy recognition by the pilot in all lighting conditions. Mechanical position indicators for both levers were placed to starboard of these handles. (Lou Drendel)

The Cavanaugh Avenger's panel contains many original instruments, with modern avionics displays confined to the starboard side of the panel. These included a GPS (Global Positioning System) receiver just above the right edge of the retracted plotting board. The Instrument Black (FS27038) panel color was authentic for US World War II-era military aircraft. (Lou Drendel)

Oxygen Regulator (Placed Behind Pilot's Seat on Bulkhead)

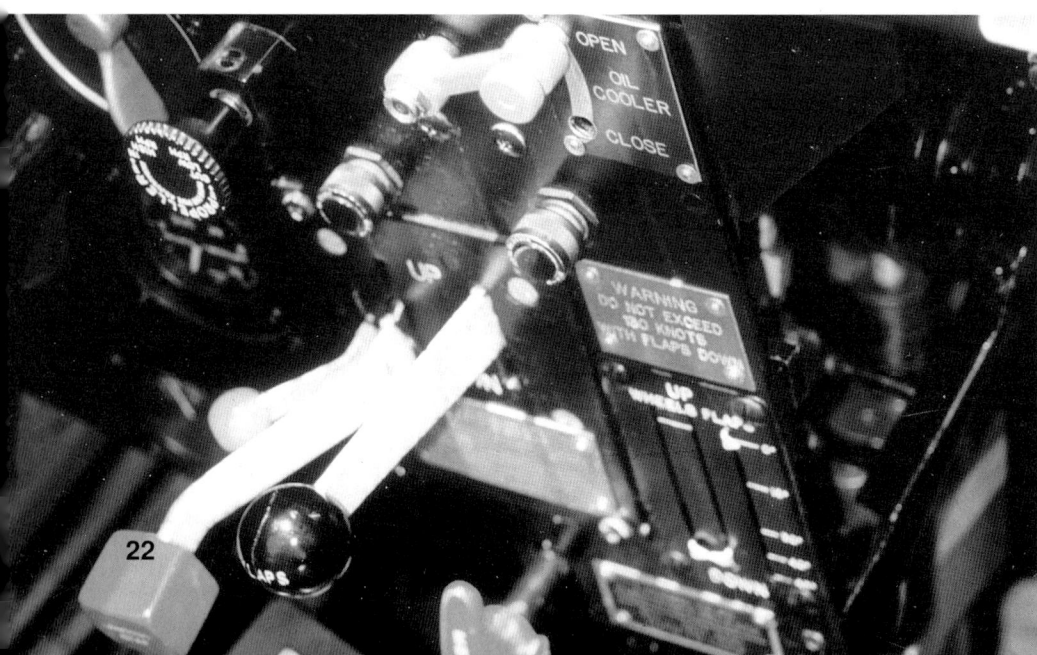

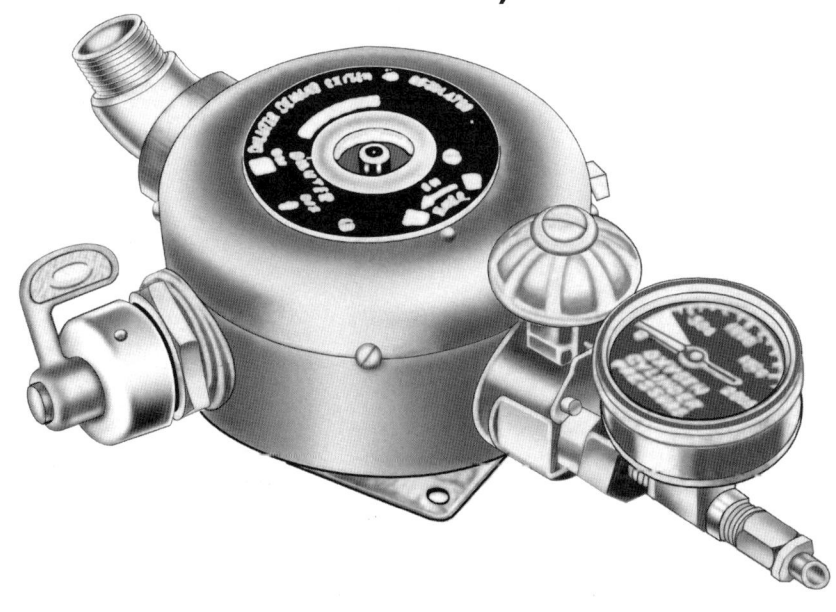

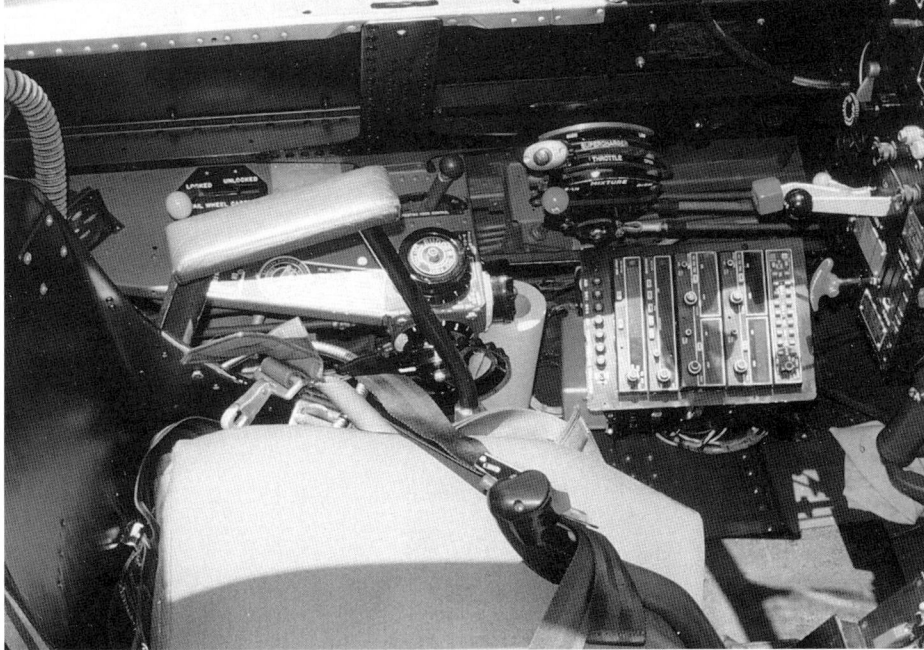

The port cockpit console of Cavanaugh's TBM-3 was painted Interior Green (FS34151), while the cockpit walls were finished in Glossy Sea Blue (FS15042) – a non-standard finish. The hose beside the pilot's seat supplied oxygen for high altitude flights. The oxygen regulator fitted behind the pilot's seat controlled the oxygen flow to the pilot's face mask. Modern aviation radios were installed beside the throttle quadrant of this flyable Avenger. (Lou Drendel)

Pilot's Seat

The Electrical Distribution Panel on the front cockpit's starboard console contained light switches, the radio master control switch, heater controls, armament switches, and circuit breakers. The Cavanaugh Avenger's panel is historically accurate. Various switches on the Instrument Black console are silver and red. The starboard rudder pedal was mounted just above the cockpit floor; the port pedal was fitted in the same way. (Lou Drendel)

The TBM (N700RW) owned by the Lone Star Flight Museum in Galveston, Texas was fitted with modern avionics and instruments. This arrangement does not resemble the original aircraft's instrument panel in any way. The control stick grip is a modern type with multiple task buttons, not the relatively simple grip used on wartime Avengers. The upper portion of the instrument panel is Flat Black, while the rest of the cockpit interior is a light blue-gray (approximately FS35526). (Lou Drendel)

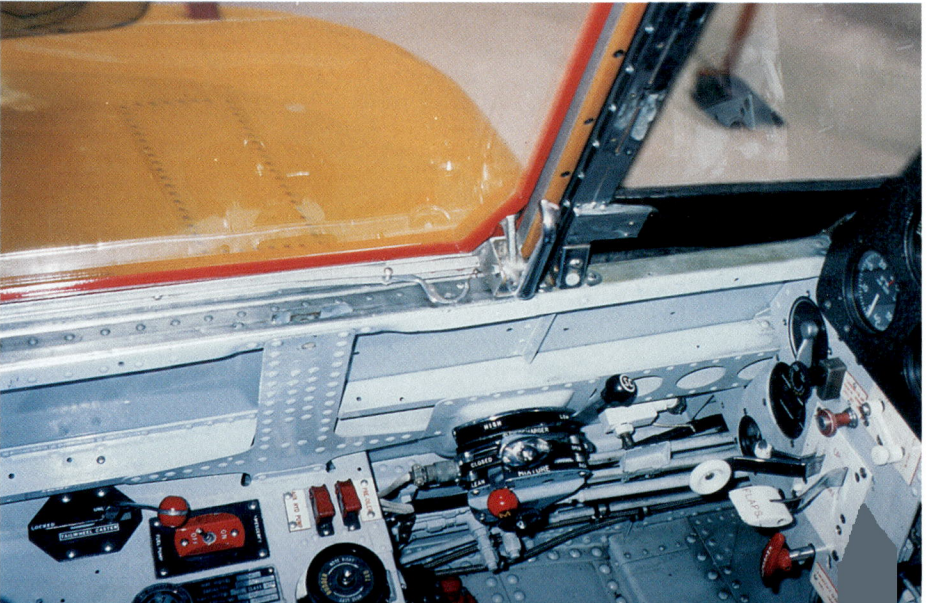

The port cockpit controls on the Lone Star Flight Museum's Avenger are in their original positions; however, the light blue-gray finish applied to this aircraft is incorrect. The round black knob on the fore end of the console was the rudder trim tab control. Below and slightly ahead of this knob – along the front of the console – was the aileron trim tab control wheel, which adjusted the TBM's aileron trim tabs as required under various flight conditions. (Lou Drendel)

The pilot's center cockpit panel on Cavanaugh's TBM-3 was retrofitted with a modern intercom panel replacing the remote indicating compass. The intercom system enabled the pilot to communicate with the other crewmen elsewhere on the aircraft. The red fuel tank selector switch enabled the pilot to select one of the Avenger's fuel tanks to draw fuel from to keep the aircraft in proper trim. Red switch covers were placed over the three fuel pump switches. (Lou Drendel)

A roll-over crash pylon was mounted immediately aft of the pilot's seat to absorb any likely loads in the event the Avenger overturned on the ground. Early TBF-1s had basic flight instruments mounted within the semi-circular opening in the crash pylon. These instruments were deleted from the TBF-1C and later models, with provision made for placing radio equipment in this area. (Lou Drendel)

The radio operator's chair – not standard on Avengers after the TBF-1 – was fitted to the Cavanaugh Flight Museum's TBM-3. This center cockpit restoration is close to the original, the only exception being the red modern fire extinguisher fitted along the port cockpit wall just ahead of the pilot's seat. Most Avengers from the TBF-1C replaced the chair with radio equipment; however, the British used this seat on their Tarpon (later Avenger) Mk IIs (TBF-1Cs). (Lou Drendel)

The radio operators canopy was located just forward of the Avenger's turret. The starboard and center sections hinged to port, while the left panel remained fixed in position. There were no clear panels separating the radio operator's cockpit from the aft canopy and rear turret. The canopy inner surfaces were painted Interior Green (FS34151), while the exterior surfaces were finished Glossy Sea Blue (FS15042) to match the fuselage exterior. (Lou Drendel)

The TBM-3's radio antenna mast was mounted atop the canopy, immediately ahead of the radio operator's cockpit section. The wire antenna led from the top of this mast to a short mast atop the rudder. A secondary wire antenna was usually mounted from the main wire antenna to the mid-fuselage just ahead of the turret. The Avenger was equipped with an AN/ARC-1 VHF (Very High Frequency) radio, which had nine main channels (frequencies) and one guard (emergency) channel. (Lou Drendel)

The access door to the navigator/bombardier compartment was immediately starboard of the radio operator's seat. The radio operator passed through the doorway, crawled past the turret, and went down into the bombardier's position during level bombing missions. This door was kept shut when the radio operator's station was relocated to the aft fuselage under the gun turret. (Lou Drendel)

The radio operator's canopy was hinged to port, with the starboard and center sections folding to allow access to and egress from the TBF/TBM's center cockpit. Entry to this station was only over the wing from the Avenger's starboard side. Piano hinges were used to join the three sections of this canopy. (Lou Drendel)

A folding door handle was mounted inside the lower starboard radio operator's canopy. The crewman turned this handle upon closing the canopy to lock this into position. Each of the individual Plexiglas canopy sections was removable for replacement if damaged. Rubber seals along the inner canopy surfaces kept water out of the cockpit. (Lou Drendel)

The Grumman-designed 150SE gun turret protected the TBF/TBM's upper rear area. This was the first operational electrically powered turret on an American aircraft and was fitted to all Avenger models except the late TBM-3R, -3S, -3U, and -3W. The 150SE's synchronized electric motors allowed the gunner to accurately train the turret and aim his weapon. (Lou Drendel)

The Avenger turret mounted one .50 caliber (12.7MM) Colt-Browning M2 machine gun, which was offset to the gunner's left. This weapon was supplied with 200 rounds of ammunition and could be reloaded with 200 more rounds at any time during flight. The machine gun's elevation ranged from -30° to +85°. The gun camera mounted in the turret's upper surface recorded firing results for later study. (Lou Drendel)

The TBF/TBM's gun turret protected the aft and side uppersurface of the aircraft from enemy fighters. A flush-mounted handhold under the turret assisted crewmen in climbing aboard the port side of the Avenger. The wingwalk areas were covered with a non-skid surface to ease the footpath for flight and maintenance personnel. (Lou Drendel)

The .50 caliber Browning M2 machine gun was offset to the gunner's left to allow space for the gunner and his sighting equipment. The gunner used a ring and post gunsight – mounted behind 1.5 inch (38.1mm) thick bulletproof glass – to aim his weapon. The machine gun was trained and fired using a pistol-grip control device mounted under the gunsight. (Lou Drendel)

The turret's circular port center section was removable for emergency ground egress. This was not used for bailout, because the gunner did not wear his parachute while in the turret. His parachute was stowed in the navigator compartment and both the gunner and the navigator bailed out through the starboard rear fuselage door. (Lou Drendel)

The vent aft of the turret allowed exhaust from the cabin heater to escape. This heater was installed in late production TBMs. The gunner operated the turret by holding down the gun handle's action switch. When this handle was released, the turret returned to the neutral position with the gun muzzle trailing aft. (Lou Drendel)

The turret operating mechanism contained interrupter cams, which activated a microswitch in the gun firing circuit. This microswitch prevented the gunner from accidentally shooting holes in the wing and/or tail surfaces in the heat of combat. The system only worked when the turret was electrically operated; any manual operation of the gun did not provide this safeguard. (Lou Drendel)

Crewmen used a hand hold below the turret and kick-in steps on the lower fuselage to climb aboard the aircraft's wing. A white diagonal line with an arrowhead at the top guided personnel in boarding the aircraft. The rear fuselage access door was placed aft of the window on the Avenger's starboard side. (Lou Drendel)

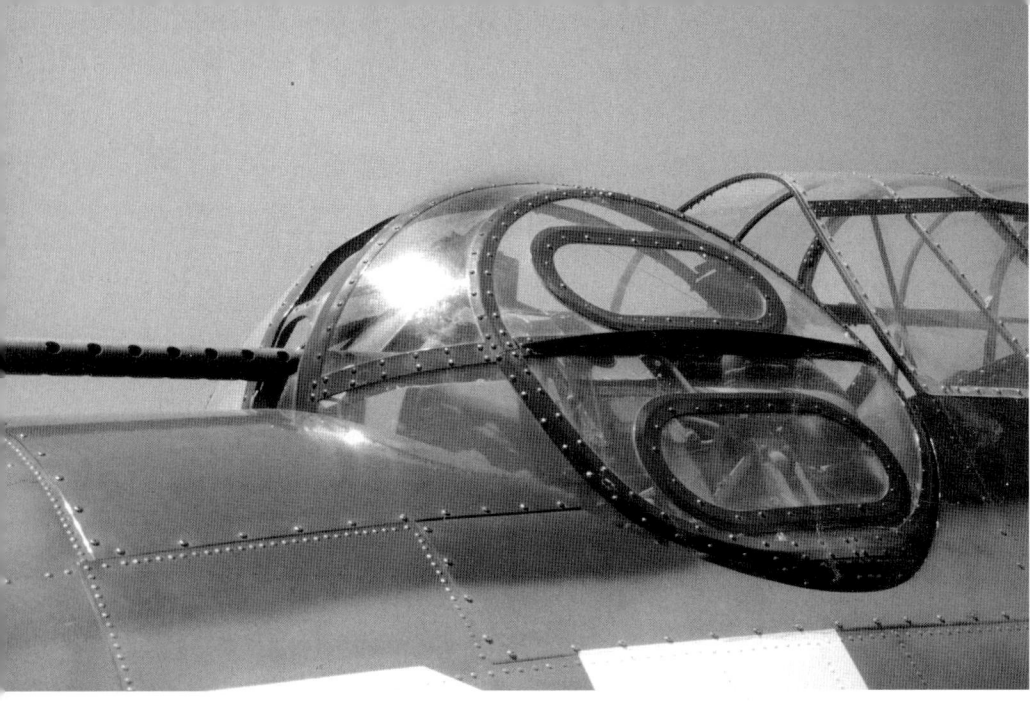

Ammunition for the .50 caliber (12.7MM) Colt-Browning M2 machine gun was stored in the turret's port side. Belted ammunition was fed through the port side of the weapon's breech and spent shell casings were ejected through a chute to a box mounted below the gun. The air-cooled M2 had a cyclic rate of 800 rounds per minute and a muzzle velocity of 2900 feet (883.9 M) per second. (Lou Drendel)

The electrically-powered Grumman 150SE turret could move at the rate of 30° per second in elevation and 45° per second in train (sideways). It was capable of training 360° and had vertical limits of -30° to +85°. The gunner was protected by armor plating, which was .5 inch (12.7MM) thick at his front, .375 inch (9.5MM) thick at the sides, and .75 inch (19.1MM) thick at the bottom. (Lou Drendel)

Grumman 150SE Turret

Front — Plexiglas Panels

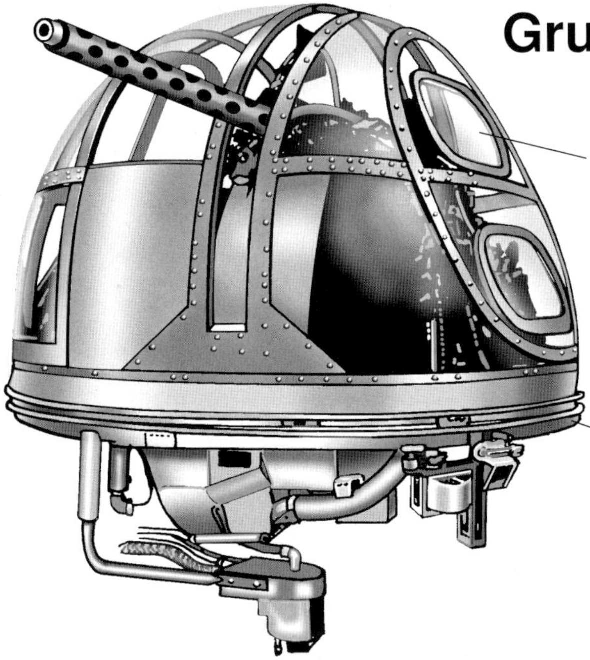

Back — Gun Camera, Bulletproof Glass, Ring and Post Gunsight, Control Box, Control Handle, Armor Plate, Armored Seat Back, Electrical Junction Box, Turret Ring, Armored Seat

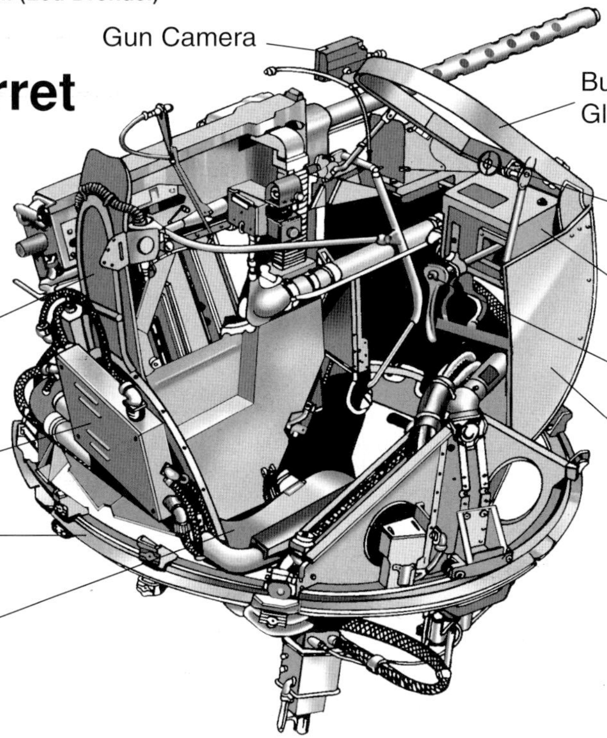

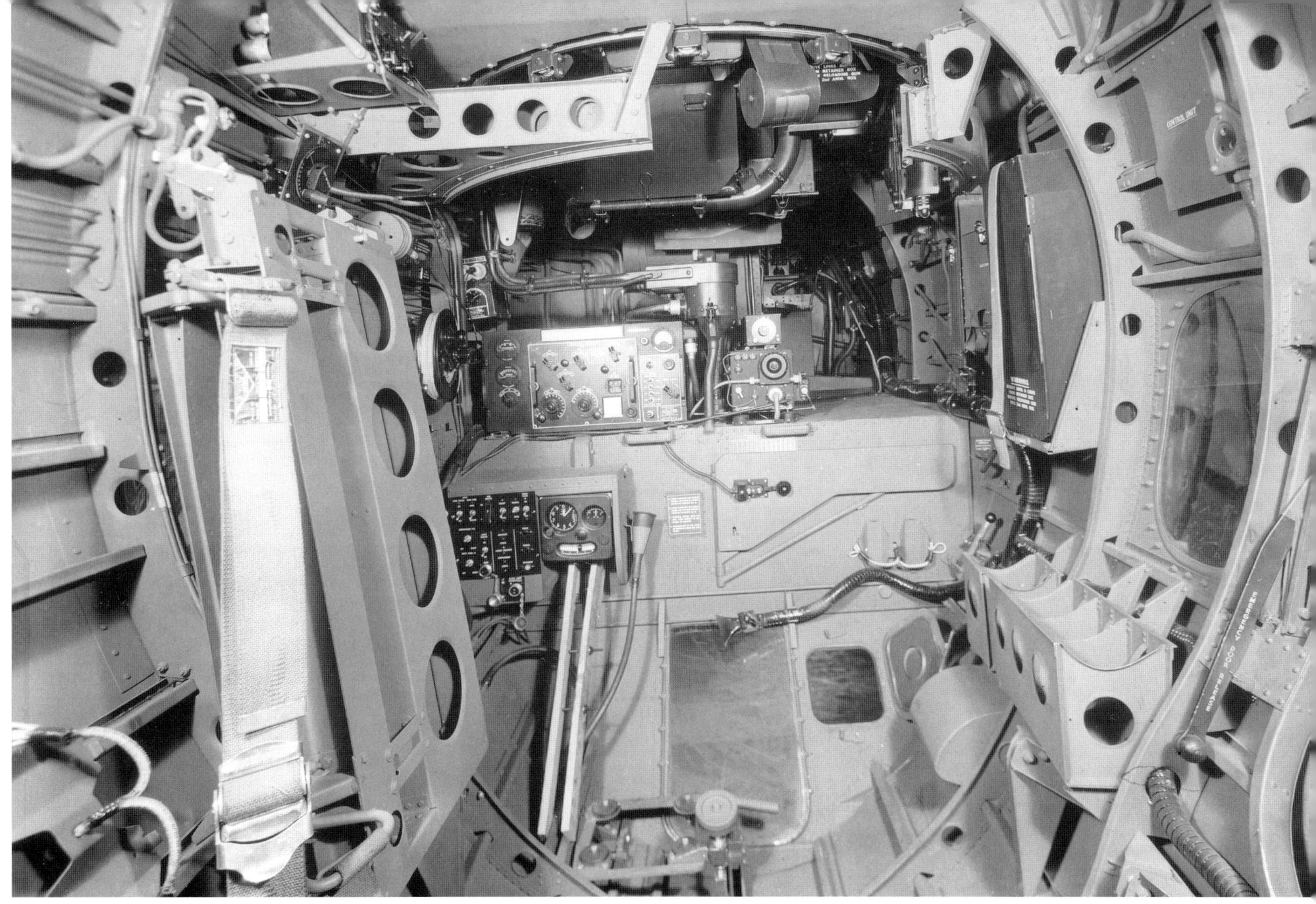

The TBF/TBM bombardier's station was located within the lower aft fuselage. The lower window – covered on the opposite side – looked into the bomb bay. The bombardier aimed through this window when the Avenger was on a level bombing mission. A radio transmitter was placed above the bomb bay window. The bombardier's centerline seat was folded to port; this replaced a port mounted seat fitted to early TBF-1s. The turret and the radio operator's position were accessed from this compartment. (Lou Drendel)

The interior of the Cavanaugh Flight Museum's TBM-3 is nearly flawless in its authentic appearance; however, the period radio equipment in the navigator/bombardier compartment is not operational. The small black box with the crank along the port wall is the intervalometer, which controlled the spacing of bombs released from the bomb bay. The bombardier set this device prior to dropping the ordnance onto the target. The overall interior finish on Eastern-built Avengers was Interior Green (FS34151). (Lou Drendel)

A red fire extinguisher – required modern flight safety equipment – was placed beside the bomb aiming window by the museum's staff. The turret gunner's lower armor plate hung from the turret position in the bombardier compartment's roof. This plate folded up when additional compartment space was needed. The starboard passageway led past the turret to the radio operator's cockpit in the fuselage's midsection. (Lou Drendel)

Brown seat belt attachments were fitted to the lower turret assembly. The canvas lap belt secured the gunner to his seat in flight. The step in the center right ceiling assisted the radio operator to climb into his mid fuselage seat. Behind this step is the turret interrupter gear, which was mounted on the turret azimuth ring. This device rotated with the turret and prevented the gunner from accidentally firing on his own aircraft. The interrupter gear replaced a cutout gear fitted to early Avengers. (Lou Drendel)

The .75 inch (19.1mm) thick lower armor plate served as a footrest for the turret gunner. His seat was also armor plated for protection from bullets and cannon shells. The silver cylinder beside the turret ring was one of the two electric motors used to revolve and elevate the turret. The turret's electric motors employed the Amplidyne form of control, which governed both the torque and speed of a motor with great precision. (Lou Drendel)

Bombardier's Seat

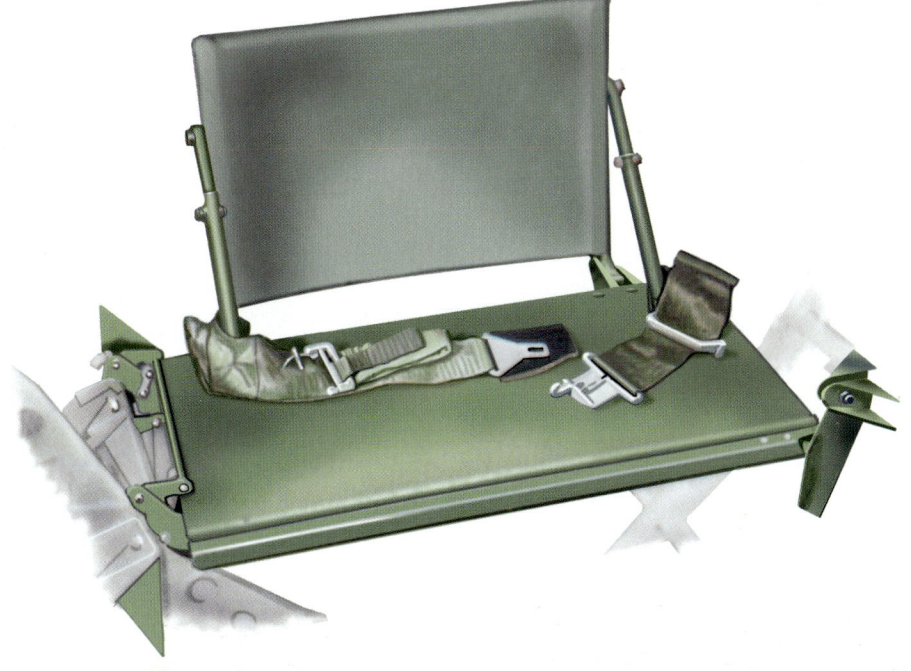

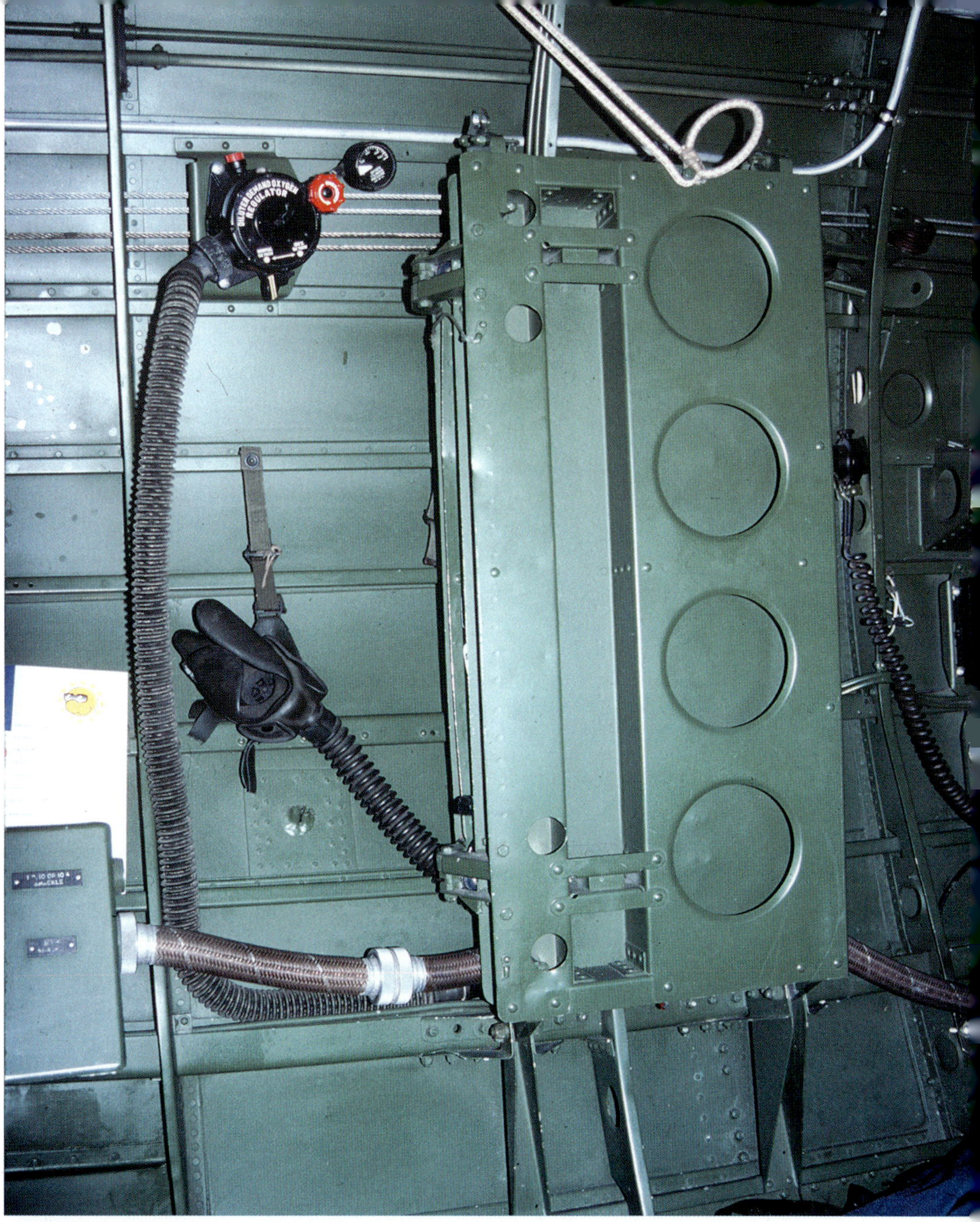

The radio operator/navigator/bombardier seat retracted to rest against the port side of the cabin wall beneath the turret. The seat back was folded forward prior to the seat being stowed. Behind the seat along the cabin wall is the radio operator's oxygen mask. This mask was connected to a hose, which was fitted to the oxygen regulator. He and the other two crewmen drew oxygen for high altitude flights from a 514 cubic inch (8422.9 cm^3) cylinder mounted in the rear cockpit. (Lou Drendel)

(Below) This restored TBM-3 was equipped with a replica .30 caliber machine gun in the ventral position. The TBM-3M model usually deleted the 'stinger' and the windows found in earlier models; this aircraft lacked the ventral side windows. The .30 caliber Colt-Browning M2 machine gun had a cyclic rate of 1200 rounds per minute and a muzzle velocity of 2800 feet (853.4 m) per second. (Glen Phillips)

(Above) This TBM-3E was assigned to the Naval Air Reserve at Cleveland, Ohio in March of 1946. The ventral 'stinger' was fitted with a .30 caliber (7.62MM) Colt-Browning M2 machine gun. The post placed on the barrel was part of the weapon's ring and post gun-sight. The radio operator manned this gun to defend the Avenger against enemy fighters from the rear and below. He fired the weapon from a hunched position in the aft fuselage gun tunnel. The sun's glare has caused the canopy to appear 'washed out.' (Warren Bodie)

Gun Tunnel

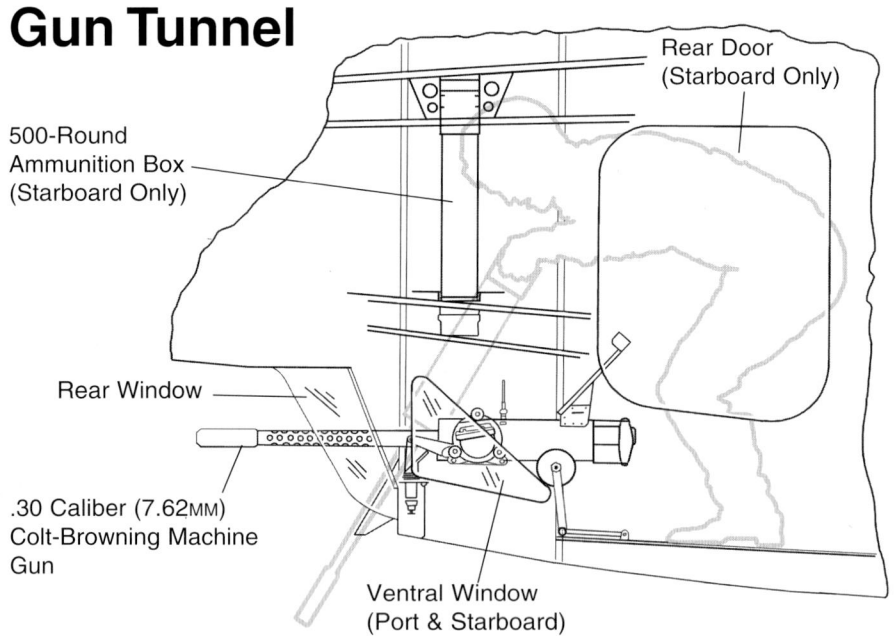

- Rear Door (Starboard Only)
- 500-Round Ammunition Box (Starboard Only)
- Rear Window
- .30 Caliber (7.62MM) Colt-Browning Machine Gun
- Ventral Window (Port & Starboard)

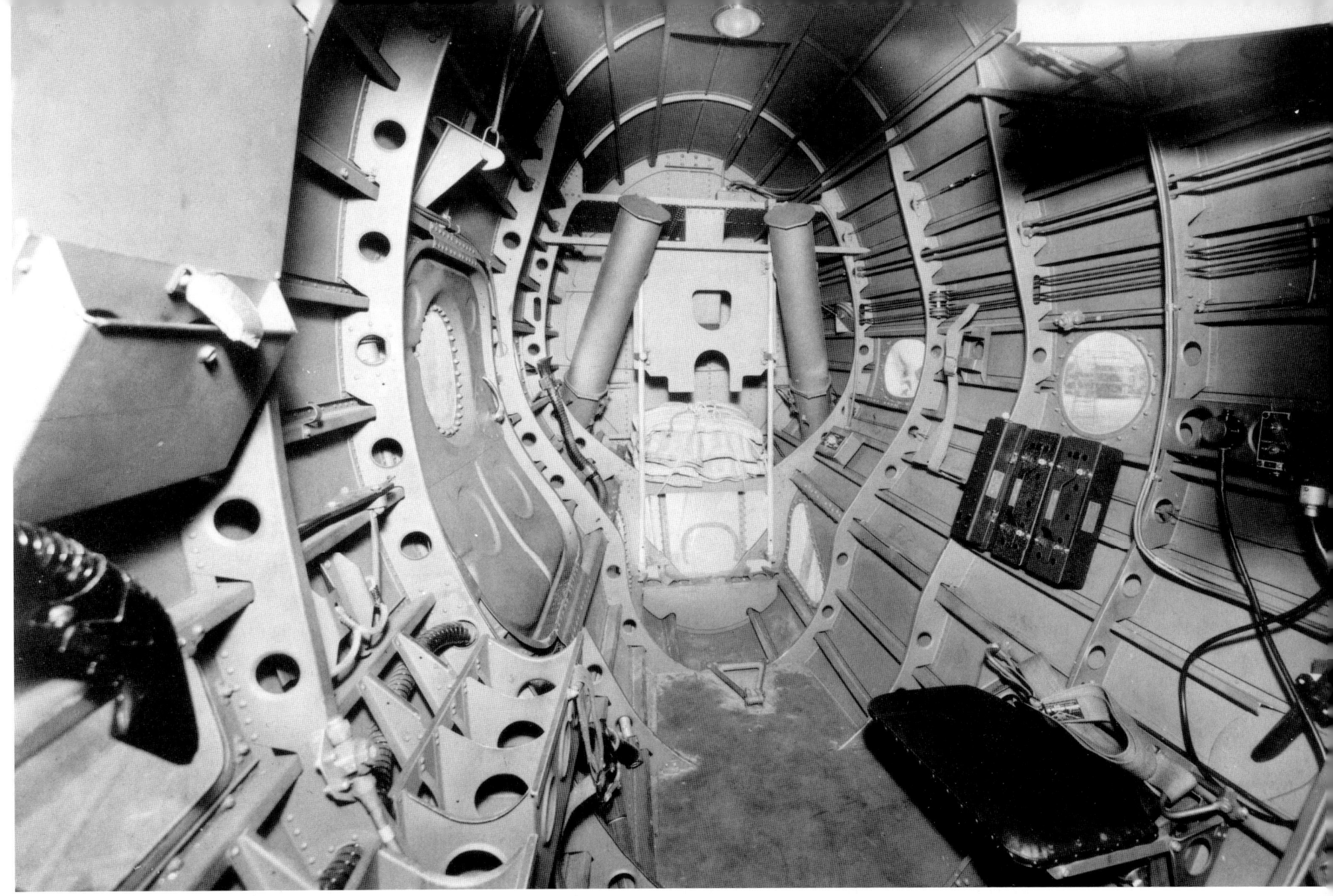

The TBF-1's ventral gun position was placed aft of the bombardier's station; this arrangement was retained in later Avenger models through the TBM-3M. The bombardier's seat was mounted on the port side on early Avengers; this was replaced with the folding seat from the TBF-1C on. The aft fuselage access door was placed on the aircraft's starboard side. The .30 caliber ventral machine gun was not installed on this Avenger and neither was the ammunition magazine usually placed on the starboard wall immediately aft of the compartment door. The two angled tubes just past the gun tunnel launched parachute flares used to illuminate the target area at night. (Grumman)

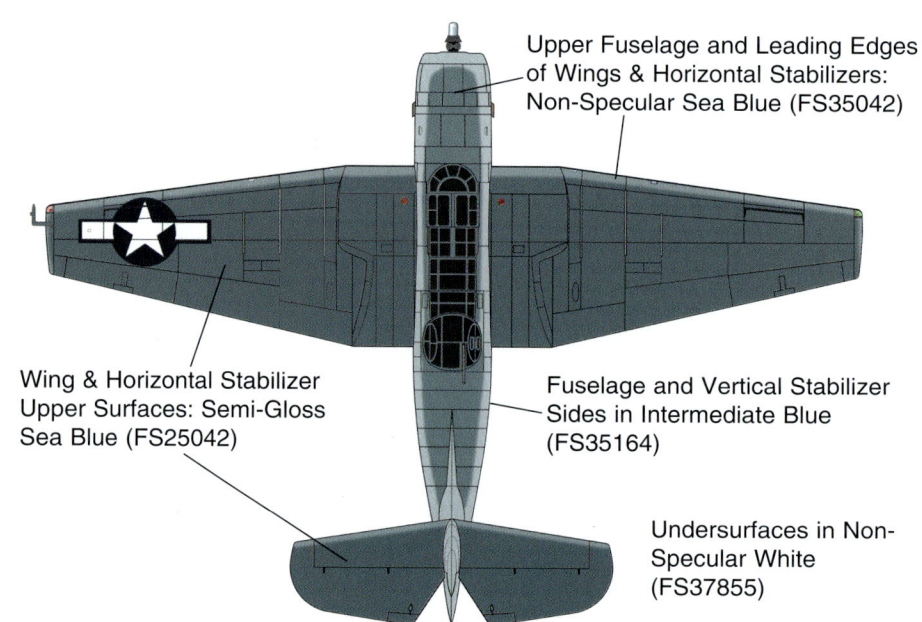

The TBF/TBM bombardier's compartment door was placed immediately aft of window on the starboard fuselage side window. Under and aft of the rear cockpit was the life raft and rescue gear storage space, which could be accessed in the event of the aircraft ditching into the water. Four replica five inch (12.7 cm) rockets were fitted to Mark 5 zero length rocket launchers under the folded starboard wing.

A restored TBM-3 – painted to resemble the TBF-1C flown by future US President George Bush during World War II – taxis at an airshow. The Avenger was painted in the three-tone Pacific camouflage finish – Sea Blue, Intermediate Blue, and Insignia White. The US Navy directed use of this aircraft scheme from 5 January 1943 until 7 October 1944; however, many Avengers and other aircraft retained this scheme well into 1945.

Three-Tone Pacific Scheme (1943-45)

Upper Fuselage and Leading Edges of Wings & Horizontal Stabilizers: Non-Specular Sea Blue (FS35042)

Wing & Horizontal Stabilizer Upper Surfaces: Semi-Gloss Sea Blue (FS25042)

Fuselage and Vertical Stabilizer Sides in Intermediate Blue (FS35164)

Undersurfaces in Non-Specular White (FS37855)

The TBF/TBM bombardier's compartment door opened forward on two flush hinges. A metal door stay was added on this restored Avenger to help the door remain open. This feature was not found on service aircraft. The bombardier/radio operator and the turret gunner could jettison the compartment door in an emergency evacuation. An emergency release lever inside the fuselage and forward of the hatch was activated to jettison the compartment door (Glen Phillips)

Overall Sea Blue Scheme (1944-1955)

Overall Finish in Glossy Sea Blue (FS15042)

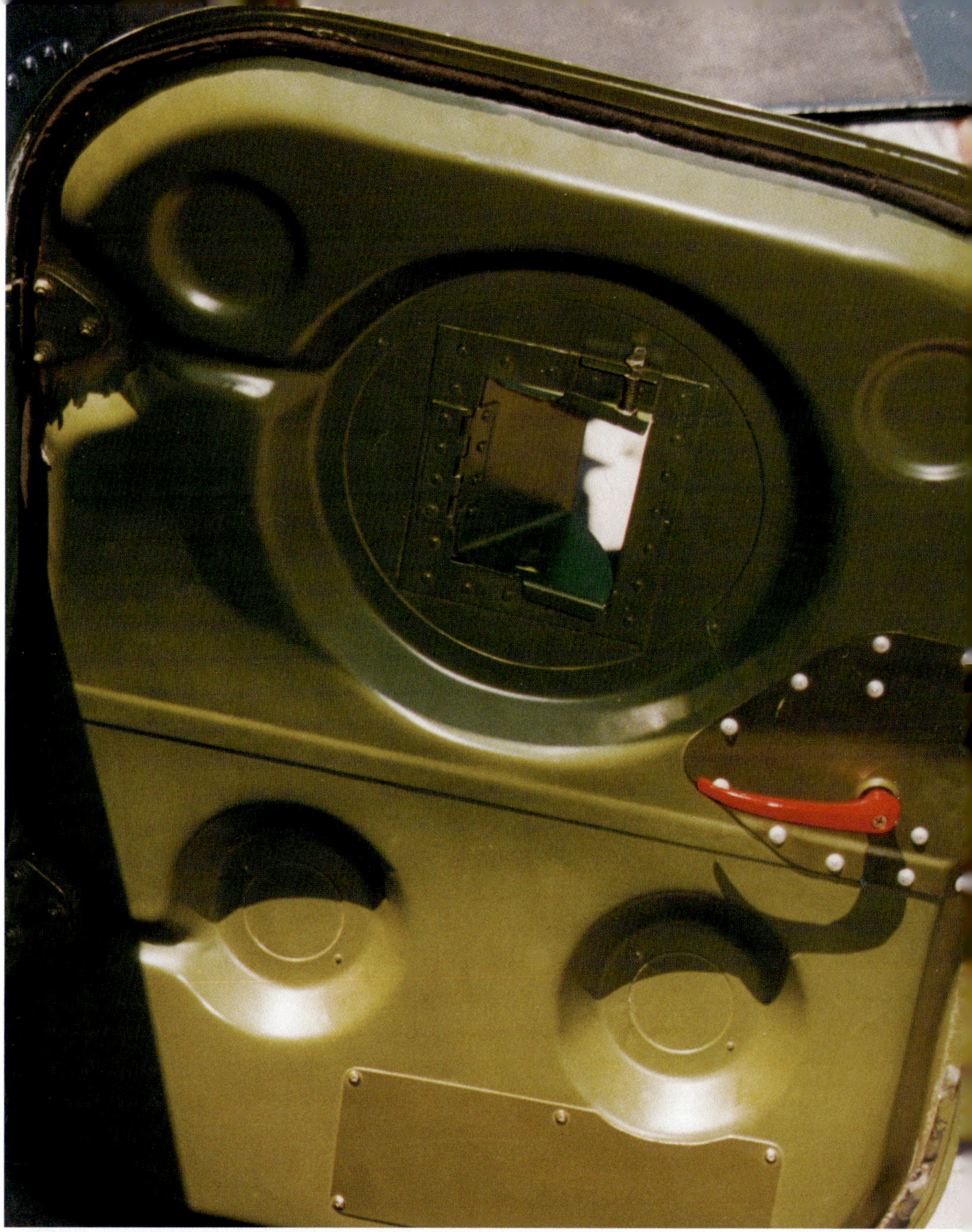

Early TBF-1s had a circular window fitted to the upper half of the bombardier's compartment door. This feature was deleted beginning with the TBF-1C; instead, a small vent could open outward. Indentations in the door's inner surface were done to create greater strength at a lighter weight than with a smooth surface. The door's interior is painted Interior Green (FS34151), with a red locking handle and black rubber seals. (Lou Drendel)

This restored TBM-3 opened its bomb bay doors for an air show display. Each hydraulically activated door consisted of two panels, with the inner panel hinged to the outer panel for folding inward. The two panels of each door were connected by cross link rods at the fore and aft ends. Two bomb host cranks were inserted into the port fuselage side of this Avenger. The bomb bay doors covered an area 16 feet 1 inch (4.9 M) long. (Lou Drendel)

Bomb Bay Door Installation

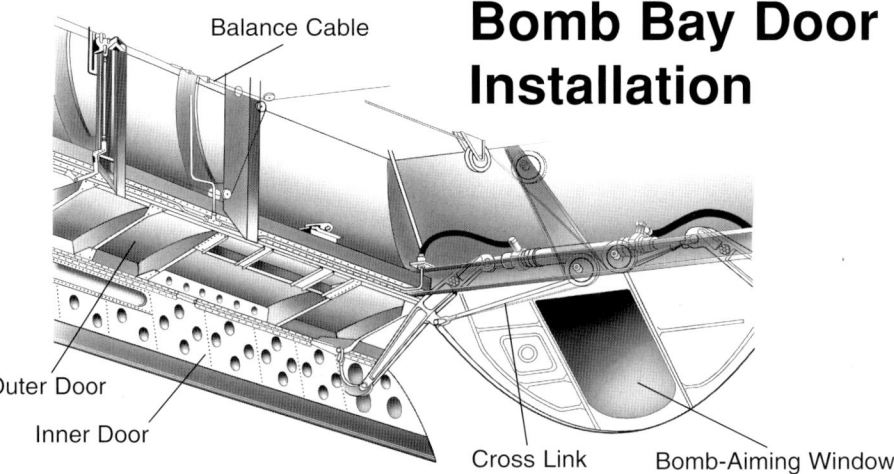

(Left) A 500 pound (226.8 KG) bomb was loaded into the TBF-1's bomb bay at Grumman's Bethpage, New York plant. A technician has begun to bring up a second 500 pound bomb into the bay using a Mark 7 bomb hoist. This hoist was inserted into a port on the fuselage side and was connected by cable with the bomb. The Avenger could carry a maximum bomb load of 2000 pounds (907.2 KG). The bomb bay could accommodate 100 pound (45.4 KG), 500 pound, 1000 pound (453.6 KG), 1600 pound (725.8 KG), or 2000 pound bombs. (Grumman)

Torpedoes Carried by TBF/TBM Avengers

Standard Mark 13

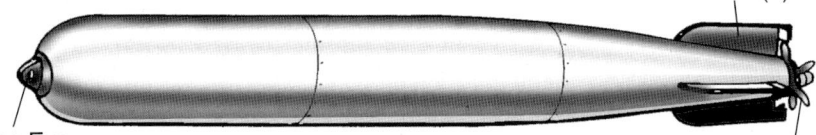

Lifting Eye — Tail Fins (4) — Contra-Rotating Propellers (2)

Modified Mark 13 (For additional stability on air delivery; wood nose & tail broke away on impact with water)

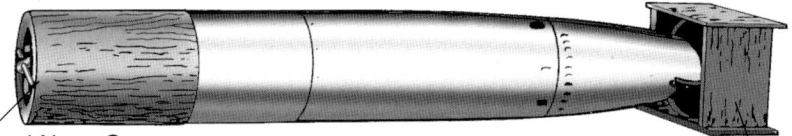

Plywood Nose Cap — Plywood Tail Fins

Mark 13-1A Ring Tail (Modified tail allowed torpedo delivery at higher speeds and altitudes)

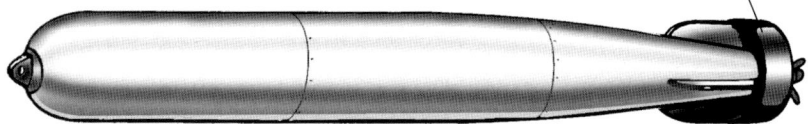

Tail Shroud

Bliss-Leavitt Mark 13 Torpedo Specifications

Width	22.4 inches (56.9 cm)
Overall Length	13 feet 5 inches (4.1 m)
Total Weight	1927 lbs (874.1 kg) in early Mk 13s; 2216 lbs (1005.2 kg) in late Mk 13s
Explosive Charge	401 lbs (181.9 kg) of TNT in early Mk 13s; 600 lbs (272.2 kg) of Torpex in later Mk 13s
Powerplant	One 98 HP (at 33 knots) alcohol-burning engine
Range	6300 yards (5760.7 m) at 33.5 knots (62.1 kmh)
Dropping Conditions	110 knots (203.8 kmh) at 50 feet (15.2 m) in early Mk 13s; 410 knots (759.8 kmh) at 2400 feet (731.5 m) in late Mk 13s

A 22.4 inch (56.9 cm) Bliss-Leavitt Mark 13 torpedo was loaded into the TBF-1's bomb bay. Two Mark 7 bomb hoists were inserted into opposite fuselage sides to lift the weapon into position. This Mark 13 was one of the early, unreliable US aerial torpedoes. American torpedoes did not become reliable until the addition of the 'ring tail' and other refinements in the Mark 13-1A of 1943. This torpedo reliability problem resulted in most wartime Avenger missions being flown with bombs. (Grumman)

This dummy torpedo was mounted in a decidedly non-standard way! The 'weapon' was secured by three pairs of canvas slings slipped to structural frames inside the bay. This TBM restoration lacked much of the bomb bay plumbing and electrical lines. The interior of this aircraft was painted Zinc Chromate primer (FS34227); however, Avengers bomb bays were usually painted Interior Green (FS34151). (Lou Drendel)

This beautifully restored Avenger's bomb bay was fitted with dummy 100 pound (45.4 KG) bombs painted black. Actual bombs were usually finished in Olive Drab (FS34087). The pilot opened the TBF/TBM's bomb bay doors using a control mounted on the lower instrument panel. Alternatively, he could throw the master armament switch to give door operation control to the bombardier. (Lou Drendel)

A pair of well-worn inert 500 pound (226.8 KG) bombs were mounted in a restored TBM-3's bomb bay. The bomb bay held either 12 100 pound (45.4 KG) bombs, four 500 pound bombs, one 1000 pound (453.6 KG) General Purpose (GP) bomb, or two 1000 pound Armor Piercing (AP) bombs. The Avenger could also carry either a 1600 (725.8 KG) or a 2000 (907.2 KG) pound bomb, or a 2100 pound (952.6 KG) torpedo. (Lou Drendel)

The port upper bomb bay door's aft section included an area marked as a step. This step area assisted personnel in boarding the Avenger over the port wing. All four bomb bay door sections – two each on the port and starboard sides – fit flush with the lower fuselage when the door was closed. The US Navy's 1939 requirement for a new torpedo bomber – met by Grumman's TBF – specified an internal bomb bay. (Lou Drendel)

A 270 gallon (1022.1 L) auxiliary fuel tank was fitted to the Avenger's bomb bay. This fuel tank was not self-sealing if hit by enemy fire and was primarily used for ferry flights. A self-sealing 212 gallon (802.5 L) tank was used for scouting missions, which extended the TBF/TBM's range to 1450 miles (2333.5 km). Both kinds of auxiliary bomb bay tanks were jettisonable in an emergency. (Grumman)

Two dummy 100 pound bombs were installed in the aft bomb bay of the Cavanaugh Flight Museum's Avenger, while a third bomb was mounted forward. The window in the bay's aft end was uncovered to allow the bombardier to aim his weapons. This window was deleted from late production TBM-3s to improve airframe strength and reduce its weight. (Lou Drendel)

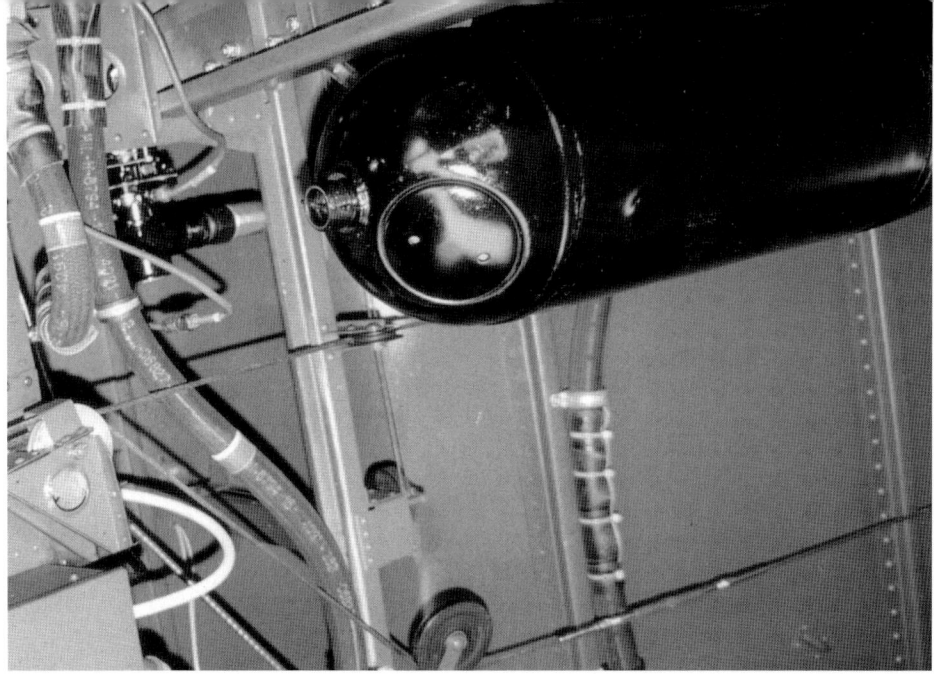

Gray hoses placed along the bomb bay's ceiling carried hydraulic liquid used to activate the Avenger's bomb bay doors. Red labels placed on the hoses indicated the use of mineral oil for hydraulic liquid. Hydraulic power was also used for the Avenger's landing gear, wing flaps and folding, cowl and oil cooler flaps, wing gun charging, and the automatic pilot. A hydraulic reservoir holding 5.5 gallons (20.8 L) of mineral oil was fitted behind the aft cockpit. (Lou Drendel)

White linen covers bundles of electrical wiring running along the ceiling of the TBM's aft bomb bay. Electrical power was primarily supplied by an engine-driven generator, with additional power coming from two batteries placed at the forward end of the bay. The brown pulley was connected with a cable used to insure proper opening and closing of the bomb bay doors. Two sets of cables ran along the port and starboard sides of the bay's ceiling. Either the pilot or the bombardier could open or close the bomb bay doors. (Lou Drendel)

Bomb Bay Auxiliary Fuel Tank

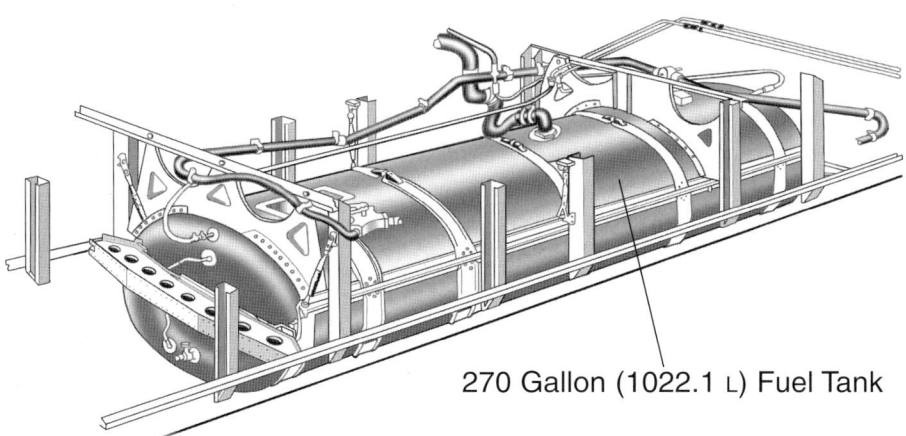

270 Gallon (1022.1 L) Fuel Tank

Mark 8 Bomb Shackle

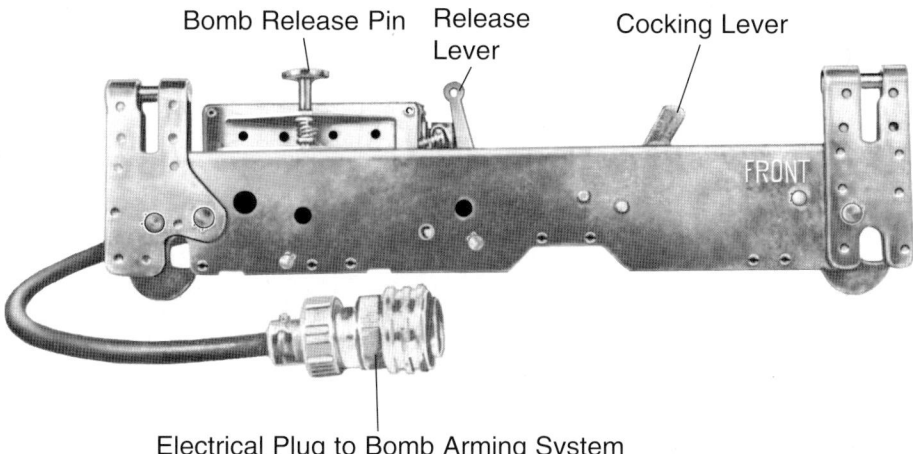

Bomb Release Pin
Release Lever
Cocking Lever
Electrical Plug to Bomb Arming System

43

Four dummy 100 pound (45.4 KG) bombs were fitted to this restored TBM-3's bomb bay. The Avenger was a deadly close support weapon during the Pacific island campaigns. Twelve 100-pound anti-personnel bombs could be released individually, all at once, or in ripple. Once the bomb drop sequence began, the doors remained open until all bombs were dropped. This aircraft's bay was painted Bronze Green (FS34058). (Lou Drendel)

Pulleys mounted above the two bombs in the aft bomb bay area guided the bay door balance cables. These cables ensured proper operation of the bomb bay doors. Additional pulleys were mounted at the front and along the sides of the bay area. Either the bombardier or pilot could release bombs from the Avenger, while only the pilot could release the torpedo. (Lou Drendel)

Lightening holes were placed in the bomb bay door inner surfaces to reduce their weight, while retaining the panels' structural strength. Hydraulic lines for bay door operation ran along the edge between the inner door and the lower bay surface. The Avenger bomb bay could also carry a smoke tank for laying smoke screens or a towed gunnery target for air gunnery training. (Lou Drendel)

The dummy 100 pound bomb fitted to this restored TBM-3 was painted black; however, actual ordnance was painted Olive Drab (FS34087). The Avenger's maximum permissible glide bombing angles ranged from 30° to 66°, depending on the size and shape of the bombs being dropped. Black rubber hydraulic lines were fitted to the bomb bay ceiling, while a door balance cable ran near the ceiling. (Lou Drendel)

A simulated 100 pound (45.4 kg) bomb was mounted in this restored TBM-3's aft bomb bay section. The bomb is secured to a Mark 8 bomb shackle, which was installed between two vertical beams running from the bay's ceiling. Bombs were released electrically from the shackles, although manual release was available in case of electrical system failure. The Mark 8 bomb shackle became standard during TBM-3 production, replacing the earlier Mark 4 bomb shackle fitted to earlier Avenger models. (Lou Drendel)

The Avenger's two 12-volt, 34 ampere batteries were fitted to the lower forward bomb bay area, on the port and starboard sides below the forward bulkhead. These batteries – recharged by the engine-powered generator – provided supplemental power to the aircraft's electrical systems. Electrical wiring and hydraulic hoses were placed between the batteries. (Lou Drendel)

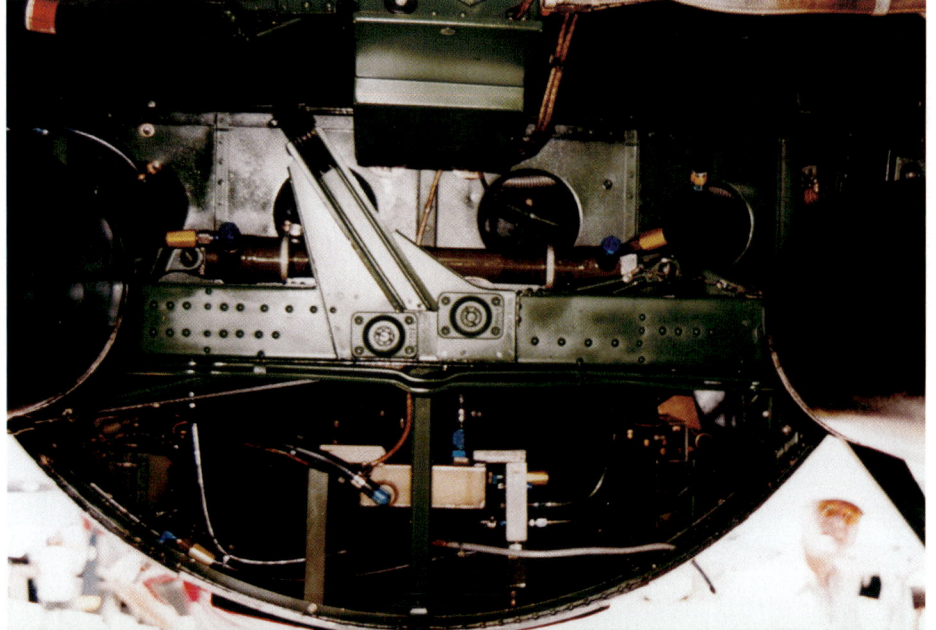

The forward bomb bay door hinge connected the lower fuselage with the inner door, while another hinge connected the inner and outer door sections. The aft bomb bay door hinge was similar in design, although modified to accommodate the angled aft door area. Rubber seals along the doors' edges kept dust and water out of the enclosed bomb bays during flight. (Lou Drendel)

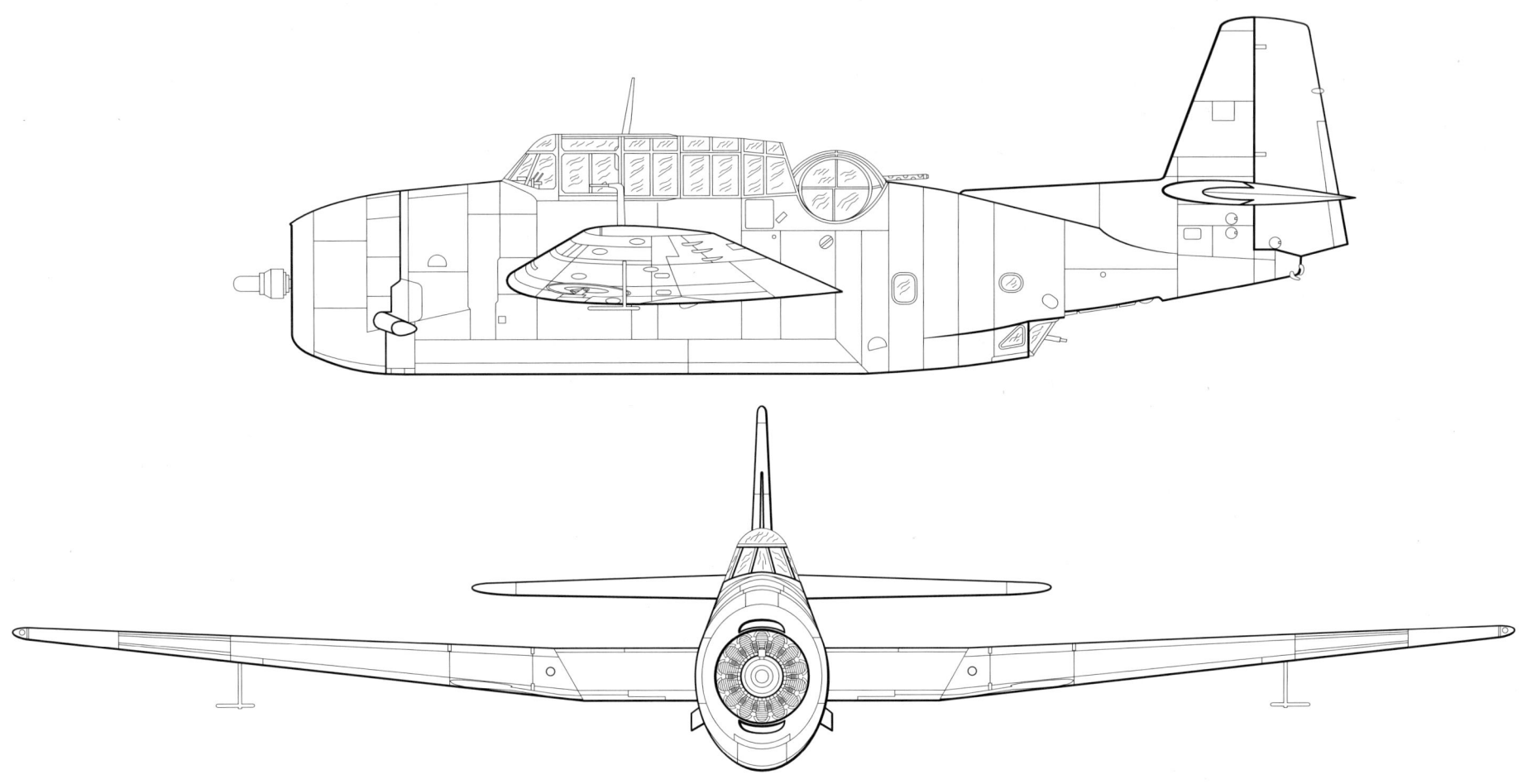

Eastern Aircraft TBM-3 Avenger Specifications

Wingspan......................54 feet 2 inches (16.5 M)
Length..........................40 feet (12.2 M)
Height..........................16 feet 5 inches (5 M)
Empty Weight................10,843 pounds (4918.4 KG)
Maximum Weight..........18,250 pounds (8278.2 KG)
Powerplant....................One 1900 HP Wright R-2600-20 Cyclone 14-cylinder, air-cooled, radial engine
Defensive Armament....Two wing-mounted .50 caliber (12.7MM) Colt-Browning M2 machine guns with 335 rounds per gun (RPG); one turret-mounted .50 caliber Colt-Browning machine gun with 400 rounds; and one ventral .30 caliber (7.62MM) Colt-Browning M2 machine gun with 500 rounds.
Offensive Armament.....One 22.4 inch (56.9 CM) Bliss-Leavitt Mark 13 torpedo or maximum of 2000 pounds (907.2 KG) of bombs or depth charges in bomb bay. Eight wing-mounted 5-inch (12.7 CM) rockets.
Maximum Speed............267 MPH (429.7 KMH) at 16,000 feet (4876.8 M)
Service Ceiling...............23,400 feet (7132.3 M)
Maximum Range............1130 miles (1818.5 KM) with torpedo; 1920 miles (3089.9 KM) as scout.
Crew..............................Three

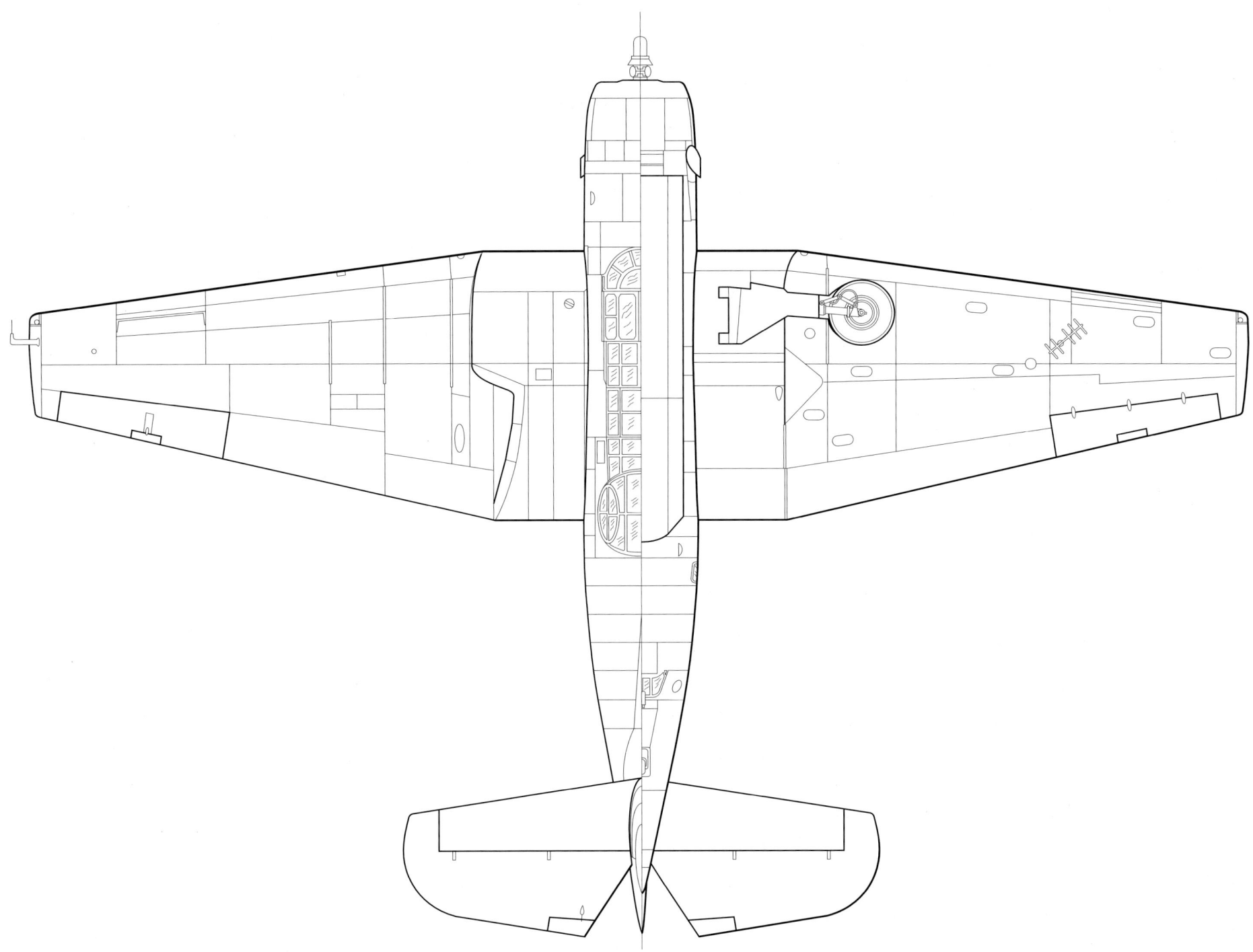

(Above) A replica 500 pound (226.8 kg) GP (General Purpose) bomb was loaded into the port aft bomb bay area of this TBM-3. The bomb casing was painted Olive Drab (FS34087) with light yellow trim. Actual GP bombs would have fuses mounted on the nose and tail, which were usually installed before the ordnance was loaded aboard the aircraft. These propeller-driven fuses armed the bomb shortly after release from the aircraft. Armor Piercing (AP) bombs – primarily used to attack surface ships – had only the tail fuse fitted. The nose fuse was displaced by the AP bomb's pointed nose for improved penetration of armor plating. The bombardier's aiming window was blanked off on this aircraft, a common occurrence on late production TBM-3s. (Glen Phillips)

(Left) The oil cooler vent was common to all TBF/TBM models, including this TBM-3. This vent extended under the fuselage immediately ahead of the bomb bay. A small flap controlled the flow of hot air coming from this vent. Two simulated 500 pound bombs were installed in the forward bomb bay area of this restored Avenger. The lifting lugs on each bomb's center section were repeated on the opposite side of the weapon. The lug was used as a hoisting point for lifting the bombs up into the bomb bay and for a fastening point with the bomb shackle. Multiple numbers of bombs were released in a sequence from the TBF/TBM's bomb bay. The bombardier set this sequence in the intervalometer located in the radio operator's compartment. The intervalometer was activated by either the pilot hitting his bomb release button or the bombardier using his firing key. (Glen Phillips)

(Above) The starboard side bomb bay doors were deployed in the full open position on this restored TBM-3E. The outer door rested in a near-horizontal position, while the inner door was angled inboard. Holes in the aft inner door end plate served to lighten the structure's weight without compromising the door assembly's strength. This aircraft was finished in overall Glossy Sea Blue (FS15042), which became the standard color for US Navy Avengers in October of 1944. (Lou Drendel)

(Above Right) The bomb bay doors were opened on this TBM-3 owned by the Lone Star Flight Museum. The oil cooler vent was placed immediately in front of the bomb bay, with the port engine exhaust pipe placed above the vent. The excess oil dump vent was located on the lower engine cowling surface, ahead of and below the exhaust pipe. The bomb bay interior was painted Gloss White, which was not found on wartime US Navy TBMs. The museum's Avenger was painted in the colors assigned to utility and target tug TBMs in post-World War II service. This scheme used Glossy Sea Blue for the fuselage, with Glossy Orange Yellow (FS13538) wing and tail surfaces. The rudder and the wing bands were Glossy Insignia Red (FS11136). (Glen Phillips)

(Right) The forward bomb bay door actuating lever was connected to the inner door, which was hinged with the outer door. The aft door actuator was similar in appearance and operation. The Avenger was the US Navy's first shipboard aircraft equipped with an internal bomb bay. The Vought XTBU-1 Sea Wolf – loser to the Grumman XTBF-1 in the 1939 USN torpedo bomber competition – also had a bomb bay. (Glen Phillips)

Armorers load 500 pound (226.8 KG) bombs onto a TBF-1 Avenger at an unidentified Pacific base on 24 July 1943. Each bomb was fused and brought to the aircraft on a small trailer, which was wheeled to the TBF's bomb bay for loading. Avengers played a pivotal role in the island-hopping campaigns in the Pacific, providing effective ground support for Allied troops. (Norman E. Taylor Collection)

A TBM-3E equipped with an AN/APS-4 search radar under the starboard wing taxis at Westchester County Airport, New York in 1946. The pitot tube fitted to all Avenger models was located on the upper port wing tip. This tube fed pitot and static pressures directly to the airspeed indicator, altimeter, and vertical speed indicator. Electrical heating elements in the tube prevented the formation of ice, which would otherwise result in false readings for the pilot. (Ed Deigan via Warren M. Bodie)

A TBM-3E was parked with its wings folded in 1946. Grumman's wing folding system reduced the wingspan without increasing the aircraft's height, which provided for easier storage aboard aircraft carriers. The wingtip tie-back cable was secured to the horizontal stabilizer to prevent the wing from inadvertently unfolding. (Ed Deigan via Warren M. Bodie)

This TBM-3C (BA-284, BuNo 85781) was fitted with four 70 inch (177.8 CM) long Mark 4 rocket launch rails under each wing. These rails – first installed on TBF/TBM-1C aircraft – held four 3.5 inch (8.9 CM) diameter rockets for use against surface targets. The British-designed Mark 4 rails were primarily used on Avengers assigned to anti-submarine duties in the North Atlantic during World War II. (Norman E. Taylor Collection)

The Mark 5 zero length rocket launcher consisted of four posts mounted on a forward plate and four posts mounted on an after plate. Both plates were secured to the outer wing undersurface with screws. The Mark 5 offered reduced drag compared to the earlier Mark 4 launch rails. Avengers could mount four 5-inch (12.7 CM) HVARs (High Velocity Air Rockets) under each wing, which were fired in pairs – one from each wing – to avoid asymmetrical loads on the aircraft. (Lou Drendel)

The HVAR's front section rested against the bottom of the Mark 5 launcher's forward post. The slot in the post's lower front section held the rocket's forward mounting lug. The California Institute of Technology developed both the Mark 5 zero launcher and the 5-inch HVAR during World War II. (Glen Phillips)

The rocket's aft section was fastened to the Mark 5's aft post, with the HVAR's aft mounting lug fitting into the lower forward section of the post. The bulge on the post held the socket for the rocket ignition wire, which was fed into the rocket motor to electrically launch the HVAR. (Glen Phillips)

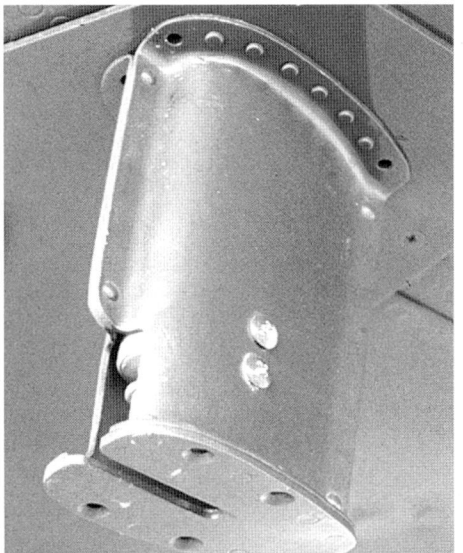

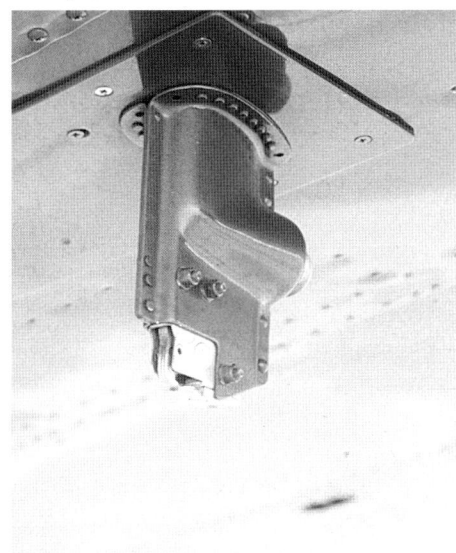

Two 5-inch HVAR replicas were mounted to the folded port wing of this restored TBM. These rockets – painted black with yellow noses – were fitted to Mark 5 zero length launchers. Actual HVARs weighed 140 pounds (63.5 KG) each, measured 72 inches (182.9 CM) in length, and had an effective range of 400 yards (365.8 M). The rockets were aligned parallel to both the fuselage centerline and the aircraft's line of thrust. (Lou Drendel)

A restored TBM-3 warms up its engine before taxiing at an air show. The wings were usually left extended when the Avenger operated from shore bases. The Avenger had a wing area of 490 square feet (45.5 м2), which combined with the Wright R-2600 engine to help make this aircraft one of the least difficult aircraft to land aboard a carrier during World War II. The responsiveness of the controls and the pleasant handling characteristics made the TBF/TBM popular with its pilots. (Glen Phillips)

The restored TBM-3 at Elkhart, Indiana folded its wings for display on the flight line. The large size of the Avenger's outer wing surfaces mandated the use of hydraulic wing folding, due to the inability of deck crews to manually fold these large and heavy surfaces. The TBF/TBM's 90° wing folding – which reduced the wing span from 54 feet 2 inches (16.5 м) to 19 feet (5.8 м) – allowed the Avenger to operate from virtually any escort carrier deployed by the Allies during World War II. (Lou Drendel)

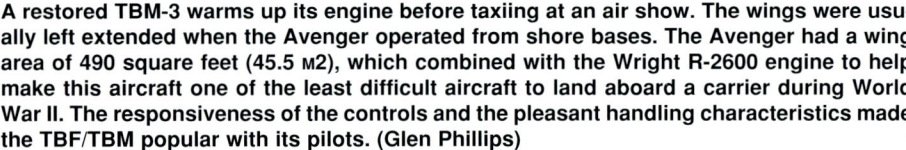

The restored TBM-3R taxis with its wings extended, either headed for the runway for takeoff or to the hardstand after landing. The dark gray surface along the wing-fuselage joint was a wing walkway covered with a non-skid finish. This finish did not appear in service until after World War II; however, it was used on post-war TBMs. Non-skid finishes provided a textured surface for personnel walking on this portion of the aircraft to have a firm footgrip. The Avenger's uppersurfaces were painted Glossy Sea Blue; however, the undersurfaces were an unauthentic Intermediate Blue. (Lou Drendel)

The wing fold pivot point was located approximately halfway through the Avenger's wing chord (width). This pivot was mounted to the aircraft's main wing spar for strength. A bolt was fitted within the cylindrical wing hinge filler block. A lubricator inside the bolt spread grease inside the hinge block to ensure its smooth operation. The outer wing sections rotated 90° along the pivot point to fold back along the fuselage sides. Steel flush screws lost their paint coverage after much unscrewing and rescrewing and displayed corrosion in comparison to the painted aluminum surface. (Lou Drendel)

The port outboard flap was opened on the folded wing of the Lone Star Flight Museum's Avenger. Lightening holes were placed in the flap's inner surface. Each TBF/TBM had two flaps per wing, one each in the outboard (folding) and inboard wing sections. The flaps had a maximum deflection of 45° for landing. Flap and flat well inner surfaces were painted red on post-World War II aircraft; wartime Avengers had these surfaces finished to match the wing color. (Lou Drendel)

A leading edge slot was fitted to the outboard wing sections of all Avengers. This slot directed smooth airflow over the ailerons, which improved their low-speed effectiveness. Each fabric-covered aileron was equipped with an aluminum trim tab, whose actuator was mounted on the uppersurface. The pilot could adjust the aileron trim tab +/-8° to insure proper aileron hold under certain air loads. (Lou Drendel)

A TBF-1 from an unidentified unit flies on patrol over the Pacific during 1944. This Avenger is equipped with the Westinghouse Air-to-Surface Type B (ASB) radar with Yagi antennas under each wing. The Yagi antenna was mounted 40° outboard, with the array of dipoles able to rotate slightly port or starboard as required. The bombardier viewed the radar returns on his radarscope, located at his aft fuselage station. ASB radar – fitted to most production TBFs and TBMs – allowed Avenger crews to attack surface targets at night and under most weather conditions. The pitot tube was mounted on an inverted L-shaped fairing placed on the upper port wing tip. (Norman E. Taylor Collection)

Air-to-Surface Type B (ASB) Radar
Fitted to Most Avenger Models

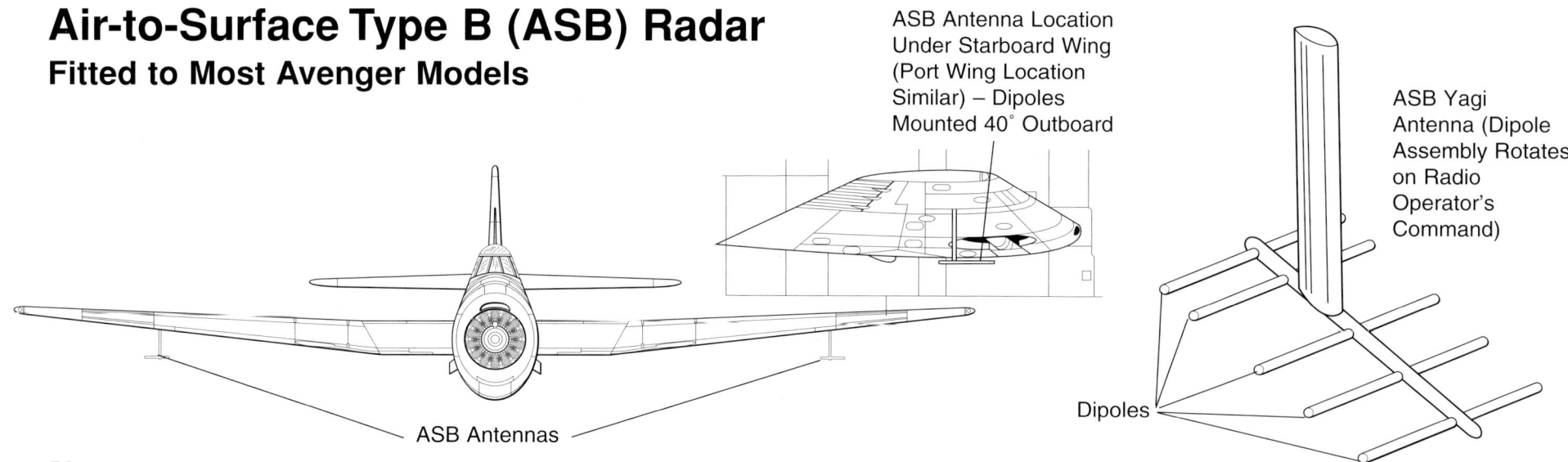

ASB Antennas

ASB Antenna Location Under Starboard Wing (Port Wing Location Similar) – Dipoles Mounted 40° Outboard

ASB Yagi Antenna (Dipole Assembly Rotates on Radio Operator's Command)

Dipoles

The Avenger's pitot tube was mounted on the port wing tip at an upward angle. This tube collected airflow for the air speed indicator in the cockpit. The tube head was left in natural metal to prevent interference with its collection capabilities. A red navigation light was mounted behind a clear housing on the port wingtip. A green light was placed in an identical housing on the starboard wingtip (Lou Drendel)

The cover placed on this pitot tube protected it on the ground from insects, which were prone to building nests inside the tube's opening. This cover was clipped over the upper portion of the tube head and was removed before flight. The wing tie-back cable was secured to the leading edge of the Avenger's horizontal stabilizer. This cable ensured that the aircraft's wings would remain fully folded back under high wind conditions. (Lou Drendel)

The metal tie-back cable was fastened to the cable enclosure located in the Avenger's wingtip. The cable loop was placed around a bolt, which was threaded through a bracket placed on the compartment's back wall. Washers separate the ribs from the cable loop. The cable was coiled inside the compartment and the two doors were fastened shut when this cable was removed from the horizontal stabilizer. (Glen Phillips)

The wingtip tie-back cable was attached to a metal loop fixed to the horizontal stabilizer's leading edge. A bolt passed through the two loops at the cable's end, which enclosed the stabilizer's anchor loop when the tie-back cable was in use. The retaining wire keeps this bolt with the cable to prevent the bolt from being lost when not in use. Deck crewmen placed the tie-down cable on the tail after the pilot had hydraulically folded the wings back following recovery aboard the carrier. (Glen Phillips)

The wing tie-back cable enclosure consisted of upper and lower doors, which conformed to the wingtip's shape and size. These doors were secured with Dzus fasteners – countersunk screws with slotted shanks used to close removable or hinged panels – when the cable was not in use. The tie-back enclosure and door inner surfaces were painted Interior Green (FS34151). (Lou Drendel)

A clear landing light with a silver back was installed in the TBF/TBM's port outer wing. This light extended down 90° when in use, with the lens facing forward. The lamp was turned on for the aircraft's approach, landing, and taxiing at night or in bad weather. The Lone Star Flight Museum's Avenger was finished in the colors of a post-World War II utility squadron. US Navy utility squadrons flew various TBF/TBM models until the last Avenger was retired from USN service in early 1957. (Lou Drendel)

TBM Utility/Target Tug Scheme

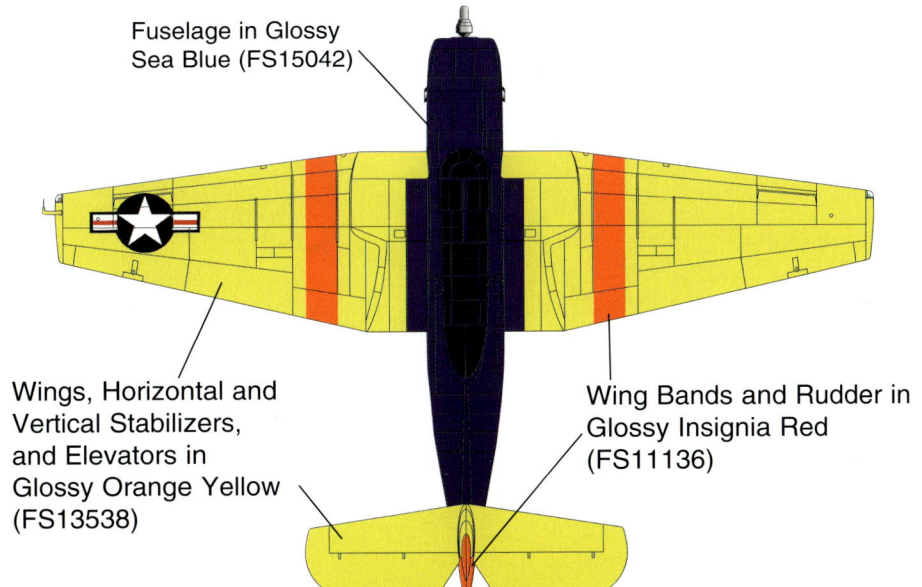

Fuselage in Glossy Sea Blue (FS15042)

Wings, Horizontal and Vertical Stabilizers, and Elevators in Glossy Orange Yellow (FS13538)

Wing Bands and Rudder in Glossy Insignia Red (FS11136)

Each Avenger's aileron had three externally-mounted hinges fitted to the wing and aileron undersurface. These hinges were connected to the control cables, which led from the pilot's control stick. The ailerons were fabric covered metal framing, with an aluminum trim tab placed on the trailing edge. Aileron deflection ranged from -19.5° to +20.5°. (Lou Drendel)

The heavy wing fold locking pin bracket was mounted in the forward inner surface of the outer wing. A bolt on the inner wing slid through this bracket to lock the wing for flight. The barrel of the .50 caliber Colt-Browning M2 machine gun protruded from the wing leading edge just outboard of the fold. Two .50 caliber weapons, each with 335 rounds of ammunition, were first installed in the wings of the TBF/TBM-1C. This arrangement replaced the TBF-1's single .30 caliber (7.62MM) fuselage-mounted machine gun. (Lou Drendel)

Wing Gun Installation

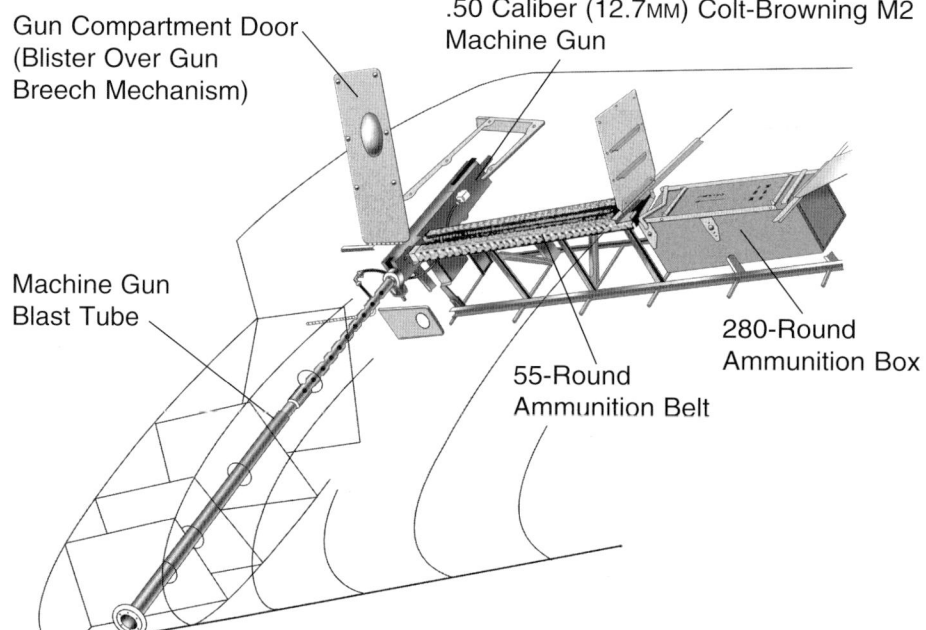

The Avenger's wing fold inner surfaces, landing gear struts, and gear door interior were painted Interior Green (FS34151) on this restored example. Landing gears on wartime aircraft were usually painted to match the undersurface color, while the wing fold inner surfaces were Interior Green. The bulge on the aft wing surface covered the breech for the wing-mounted .50 caliber (12.7MM) Colt-Browning M2 machine gun, which was introduced on the TBF-1C. (Lou Drendel)

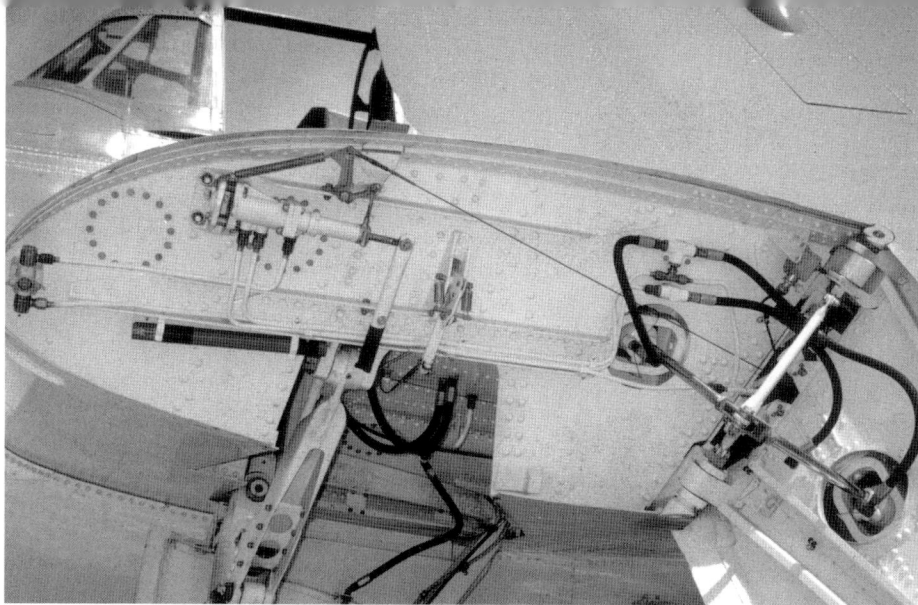

The Avenger's landing gear struts were fitted to the inner wing section. The hydraulically-operated wing fold locking cylinder was placed above and forward of the landing gear strut attachment. Grumman's unique wing fold mechanism was also used on the F4F/FM Wildcat and the F6F Hellcat. This mechanism enabled these aircraft to occupy less storage space on crowded aircraft carrier decks during World War II. The wing fold method was particularly valuable for the Avenger, which was used extensively on the small escort carriers. (Lou Drendel)

The two wing fold hydraulic cylinder rods converged at the top of the actuating link, which was connected to the wing hinge bolt. Two pulleys inside the wing hinge controlled the cable used to govern the outer wing folding movement. Black rubber hoses carried hydraulic liquid between the fuselage reservoir and the cylinders in the wings. The pilot actuated a T-shaped handle in the cockpit to lock the wings in the spread position. (Lou Drendel)

When the Avenger's outer wings were folded back, a portion of the inner wing uppersurface was exposed. The triangular sections inside the wing were stringers used to provide strength to this area of the airframe. All wing inner surfaces were painted with anti-corrosion Zinc Chromate (FS34227) paint. The lowered triangular door covered the cutout portion of the outer wing panel and automatically opened when the wing was folded. (Lou Drendel)

This restored TBM-3 was displayed with its wings folded back. A bomb rack with a simulated bomb was mounted under the inner wing section immediately aft of the landing gear. Carrier-based aircraft required strong landing gear assemblies to absorb the high stress of carrier landings. The Avenger's main landing gear was stressed for a vertical velocity of 16 feet (4.9 M) per second. (Lou Drendel)

A simulated 500 pound (226.8 KG) bomb was loaded onto the TBM-3's inner wing bomb rack. Fore-and-aft pairs of sway braces kept the bomb steady until it was released from the aircraft. This bomb rack – introduced on the TBM-3 model – was seldom used on Avengers in service, since ordnance was usually loaded into the bomb bay. A 58 gallon (219.6 L) or 100 gallon (378.5 L) external fuel tank could also be mounted on this station. (Lou Drendel)

The main landing gear for all Avenger models operated hydraulically. This unit retracted outward and upward into the wheel wells located in the outboard wing panels. The gear retraction strut was mounted to the forward gear leg and the landing gear bay. Hydraulic pressure on this strut pulled up the landing gear leg on retraction and lowered the gear leg on extension. (Lou Drendel)

The main landing gear leg bent slightly outwards approximately halfway between the wing and the wheel hub. The scissor link connecting the upper and lower gear leg sections was mounted at the front, with the oleo (shock absorbing) strut left in chrome for smooth operation. The retraction strut folded inward during landing gear retraction. A micro switch mounted just below the retraction strut section joint governed the movement of the main and retraction struts. (Lou Drendel)

Each TBF/TBM main landing gear was equipped with a Goodyear ten-ply tire, which measured 34 inches (86.4 cm) in diameter by nine inches (22.9 cm) wide. The tire pressure was 110 pounds (49.9 kg) per square inch for carrier operations and 95 pounds (43.1 kg) per square inch for operating from land. The spoked wheel disc cover allowed air to cool the Goodyear hydraulic disc brake. The disc cover was removable to allow the tire and wheel to be removed and for servicing the brake. (Lou Drendel)

The Avenger's main landing gear retracted 90° outboard to rest within the wing-mounted gear well. Hydraulic pressure acted upon the side strut, which pulled the main gear strut up on retraction and pulled the main strut down on extension. A lock was fitted within the wheel well where the side strut was mounted. This lock was automatically released when hydraulic pressure began to activate the landing gear at the beginning of both retraction and extension sequences. (Lou Drendel)

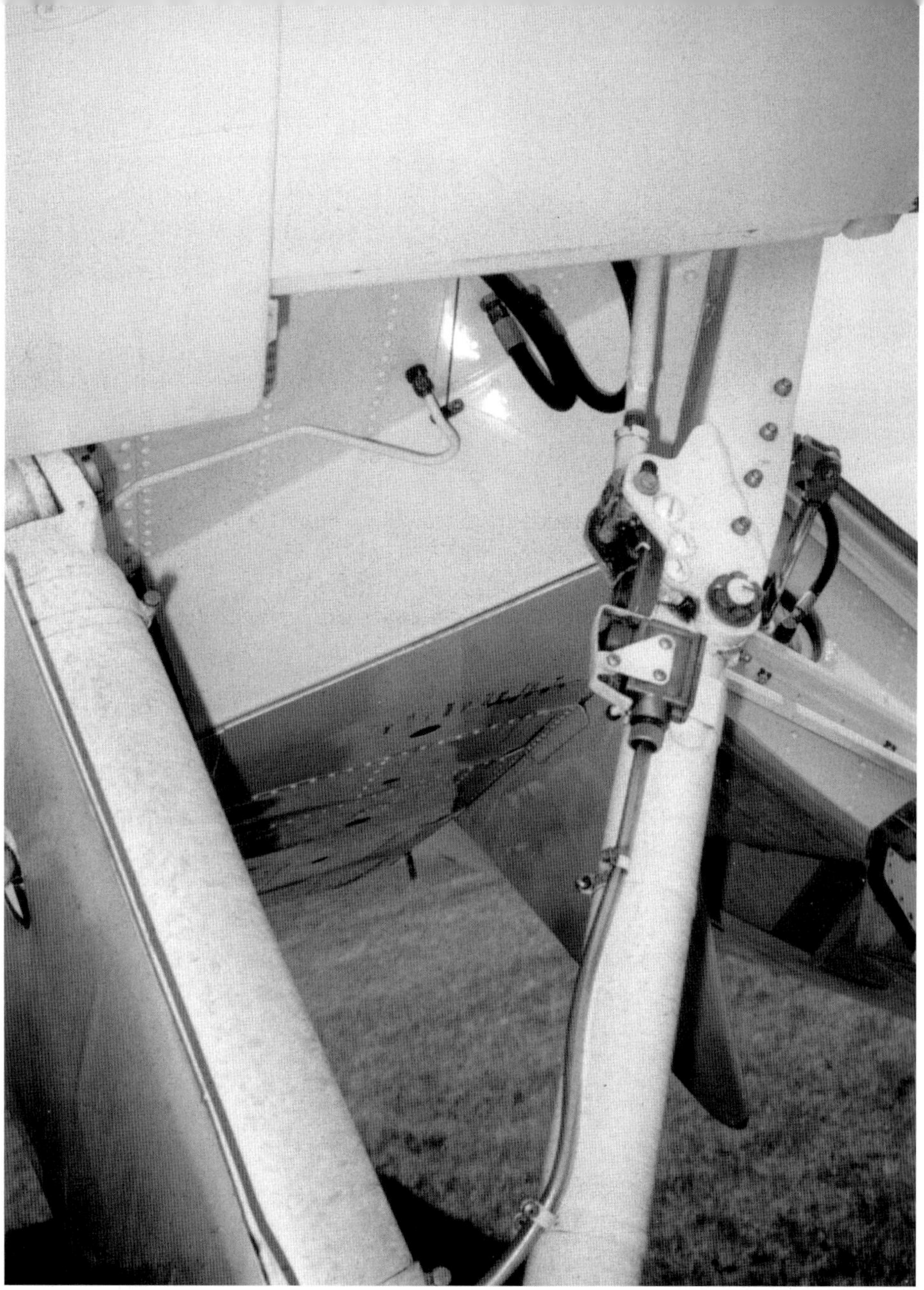

An electric microswitch was installed on the folding joint of each TBF/TBM main landing gear's side strut. This switch turned on a warning horn directly behind the pilot's headrest when the engine was throttled below 1200 revolutions per minute (RPM) with the landing gear not fully extended and locked. A cable ran along the retraction strut from the microswitch to the main landing gear leg. (Lou Drendel)

A restored TBM-3 Avenger had just taken off from Marine Corps Air Station (MCAS) El Toro, California during an air show on 27 April 1990. The main gear retracted by being pulled upward and outward into the landing gear bays placed in the outer wing sections. No doors were provided for the main gear wells in order to save weight and reduce maintenance requirements. The triangular doors associated with the wing folding system are folded into the outer wing sections, aft of the landing gear bays. (Ted Carlson/Fotodynamics)

The Avenger's main landing gear well was shaped to conform to the main landing gear wheel and door assembly. The metal fore-and-aft ribs and the stringers inside the bay provided strength to the gear well structure. Black hoses in the inboard gear well area supplied hydraulic liquid to the gear retraction system. (Glen Phillips)

The box-shaped port and starboard main gear wheel well sides simplified construction of this assembly during wartime. The rubber pad placed at the upper edge of the gear bay cushioned the main gear leg when it was fully retracted. This overall Glossy Sea Blue TBM-3's gear well was painted Gloss White. Avengers in service usually had these wells painted to match the wing undersurface color. (Lou Drendel)

Two oval windows flank the turret gunner and radio operator/bombardier's access hatch on the Avenger's starboard rear fuselage. Identical windows were placed on the port rear fuselage. This window arrangement was standardized on late production TBF-1s and continued through the TBM-3. Avengers supplied to Britain during World War II replaced the windows nearest the wing with observation domes. (Lou Drendel)

The aft fuselage air intake scoop was positioned to receive fresh air untainted with engine exhaust fumes. This feature was well appreciated by Avenger radio operator/bombardiers flying in the hot and humid tropical conditions often found during the Pacific War. TBM-3s added an air heater with a second air scoop further forward on the aft fuselage. (Lou Drendel)

An air intake scoop was placed on the upper aft fuselage of all TBFs and TBMs, immediately port of the dorsal fin. This scoop brought fresh air into the Avenger's aft compartment. The dorsal fin aided in the aircraft's directional stability and was added to the Avenger beginning with the second XTBF-1 prototype. (Lou Drendel)

The national insignia applied to this restored Avenger is incorrect in both dimension and detail. The white star points should not go all the way to the edge of the blue circle. The lifting tube's port side opening is located within the rear quadrant of the national insignia. A metal bar was placed within the lifting tube to jack up the TBF/TBM's aft fuselage for aircraft maintenance. (Lou Drendel)

This restored TBM has a short extended step fitted instead of the usual flush-mounted kickstep on the port aft fuselage, below the forward radio compartment window. Crewmen used the step and the handhold up the fuselage side to aid in climbing onto the Avenger's wing root. This arrangement also existed on the aircraft's starboard side. The area between the step and the handhold was usually marked with an upward pointing arrow: black for light colored finishes, or white for dark colored schemes. (Lou Drendel)

This restored TBM-3E does not have the ventral gun tunnel windows used on earlier Avenger models. The last production model deleted the ventral .30 caliber (7.62MM) Colt-Browning M2 machine gun and the windows associated with this position to save weight and increase airframe strength. The restorers did install a window and simulated machine gun at the tunnel's aft end. All TBF and TBM windows were made from Plexiglas, except for the turret gunner's bulletproof shield. (Lou Drendel)

65

A TBM-3 (BuNo 69768) was lashed to the flight deck of the escort carrier USS BLOCK ISLAND (CVE-106) during her shakedown cruise in late 1944. A second Avenger was spotted alongside to starboard. A deck crewman was securing mooring lines from the arresting hook housing to the tie-down points on the carrier's deck. The TBM-3's elevators were turned up, due to the control stick having been pulled back by its pilot. The BLOCK ISLAND saw action in the Okinawa campaign in the spring of 1945. The embarked Marine Carrier Air Group 1 (MCVG-1) included the Avengers of Marine Torpedo Bomber Squadron 233 (VMTB-233). (USMC via Norman E. Taylor Collection)

This restored TBM-3E (NL88HP) features the externally mounted arresting hook fitted to late production examples of this model. This hook replaced the retractable arresting hook found on earlier Avengers. The wings were folded and the wingtip tie-back cables fastened to the horizontal stabilizers. The large rudder servo and trim tabs were used to offset control pressures encountered in overcoming propeller torque at low speeds. (Walt Houghton)

The Avenger's tail wheel was fully retractable, which allowed a clear field of fire for the ventral machine gun. Land-based TBFs and TBMs used a Firestone pneumatic tire, measuring 14.5 inches (36.8 CM) in diameter by five inches (12.7 CM) wide. This tire was inflated to 95 pounds (43.1 kg) per square inch. Carrier-based aircraft used a solid rubber Grizzly tail wheel of the same size. (Glen Phillips)

Coke Stuart's TBM-3E (RR-125, BuNo 85794) was finished in the colors it wore when it flew combat missions from the USS YORKTOWN (CV-10) in the summer of 1945. This Avenger flew 11 combat missions while assigned to Torpedo Squadron 88 (VT-88) aboard the YORKTOWN. The aircraft was fitted with the retractable arresting hook, which was replaced with the external hook on late production TBM-3Es. (Lou Drendel)

The TBM tail landing gear consisted of a self-aligning, full swivel type tail wheel with a controllable non-swivel lock mechanism, a Bendix Pneudraulic (pneumatic and hydraulic) shock strut, and a tire and wheel assembly. The white bracket above the tire was the fitting for the hold back cable used when catapulting the Avenger from a carrier. The landing gear strut and door inner surface – finished Bronze Green on this example – was painted on service aircraft to match the Avenger's undersurface color. (Lou Drendel)

Late production TBM-3Es – beginning with BuNo 86175 – were fitted with an external arresting hook, replacing the retractable unit installed on earlier Avengers. The external hook's fixed attachment point offered a sturdier mount, which was less prone to failure than the sliding arresting hook installation. Maintenance was easier and the corrosion risk was reduced with the externally-mounted hook. (Lou Drendel)

The tail landing gear included a two-pronged drag strut mounted beside the gear door, with a centering unit placed above the drag strut. These struts and the Bendix shock strut mounted aft were connected to the castor assembly in which the tail wheel was mounted. The shock strut pulls the tail landing gear fully up into the aft fuselage on retraction. The tail gear door covered only the landing gear strut, not the tail wheel. (Glen Phillips)

The tail hooks on US Navy carrier-based aircraft were usually striped black and white to improve their visibility for deck crews. A white navigation light was mounted immediately above the tail hook. This light enabled other pilots to determine the aircraft's position at night. A red and white control lock placed at the rudder's base prevented the rudder from moving freely in the wind while parked. (Lou Drendel)

This restored TBM-3E (BuNo 53522, NL88HP) displays a white arrowhead on the rudder. This insignia was applied to Avengers assigned to Composite Squadron 8 (VC-8) aboard the USS NEHENTA BAY (CVE-74) in early 1945. The Avenger and most other World War II-era aircraft had fabric rudders, elevators, and ailerons. The TBM's rudder had a range of 24° to either port or starboard. The white area under the horizontal stabilizer's base provided counter shading as part of the camouflage scheme. (Walt Houghton)

The inscription INSERT PIN TO LOCK WING on the horizontal stabilizer's leading edge referred to the ability to lock the folded wing against the stabilizer to prevent wind damage. Immediately above this inscription was the tie-back cable anchor point. The Avenger's elevators had a movement range from +20° to -10°. (Lou Drendel)

Each elevator was fitted with two hinges mounted on the elevator spar. These hinges were attached to the elevator spar and rotated on brackets fitted to the horizontal stabilizer. The elevator control unit was placed between the horizontal stabilizers' root. The horizontal stabilizer skins were aluminum alloy, while the elevator was fabric covered. (Lou Drendel)

One of the advantages of fabric covered control surfaces is the ability to repair holes with duct tape! The tape repaired a hole immediately under the rudder servo tab horn. This horn and the horn for the trim tab immediately below were only on the rudder's starboard side. Control horns provided aerodynamic force to aid in the deflection of the tabs. This aircraft is the combat veteran TBM-3E (RR-125, BuNo 85794), owned by Coke Stuart. (Lou Drendel)

Avengers were equipped with aluminum split rudder tabs. The servo tab at the top generated the aerodynamic force required for moving the rudder port or starboard. The trim tab immediately below the servo tab was used to counteract aerodynamic forces. This trim tab moved opposite the direction of rudder deflection and served to 'boost' the rudder, easing its use for the pilot. (Lou Drendel)

The rounded leading edge of the rudder allowed for ease of movement when deflected to either port or starboard. The tab flex shaft running from the vertical stabilizer's base carried input from the pilot's rudder trim controls to the trim tabs. The rudder control cable ran along a grooved wheel at the rudder's base and through the vertical stabilizer. A red and white striped rudder lock was installed on this parked Avenger. (Lou Drendel)

A fairing immediately below the base of the rudder held the TBF/TBM's retractable arresting hook. The arresting hook was deployed electrically, with the hook slid back on a chain-driven sprocket gear system. The Avenger's tail hook could move 15° to either port or starboard and hung down at a 55° angle. The pilot retracted the hook after recovery aboard the carrier. A white formation light was mounted immediately above the tail hook. (Lou Drendel)

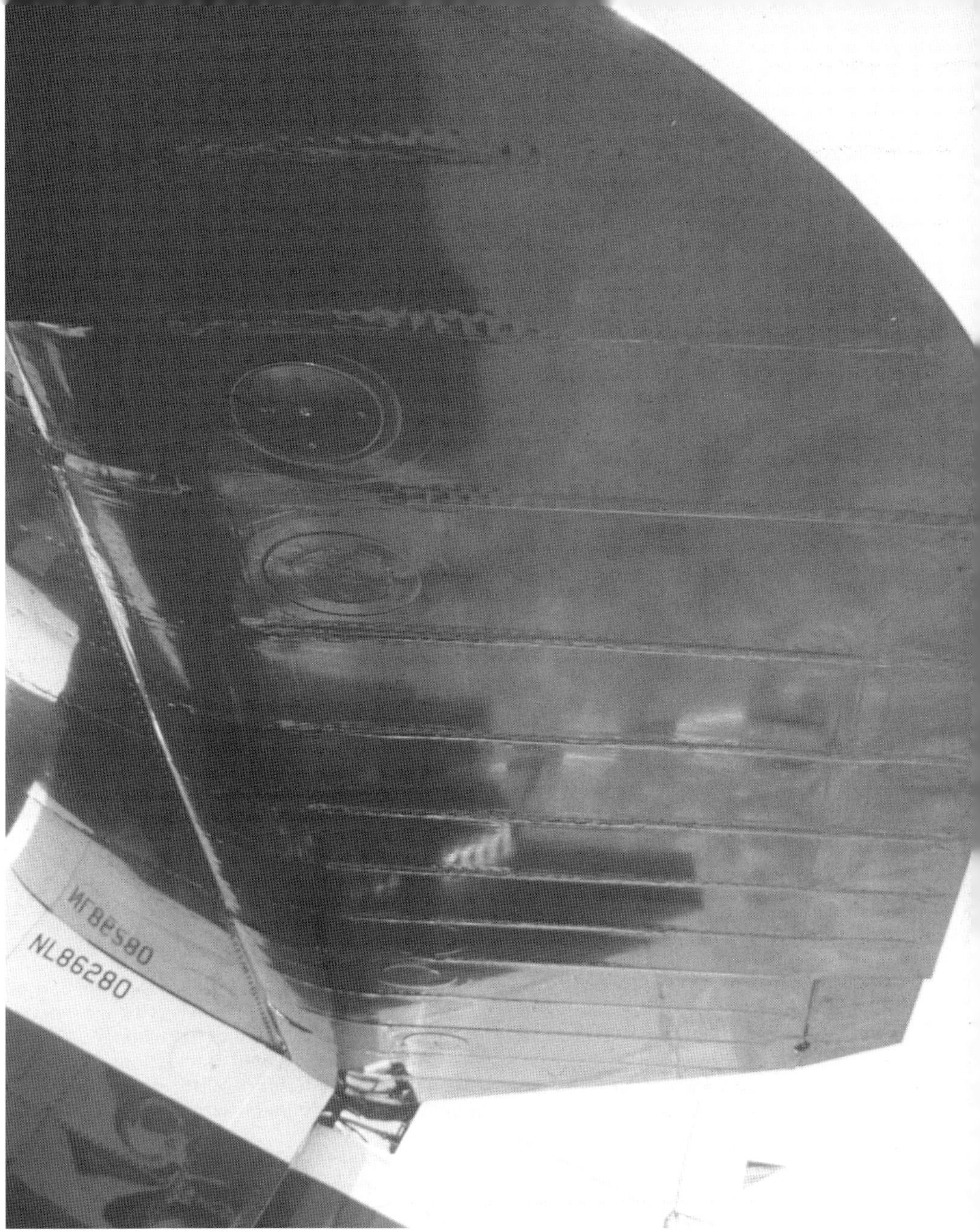

Round inspection plates placed near the elevator's leading edge allowed access to the control surface's main spar. Similar plates were also placed on the Avenger's rudder. The fabric covering stretched tightly over the metal control surface frame. The aluminum elevator trim tab was mounted on the inboard trailing edge. The port elevator trim tab's actuator was mounted on the uppersurface, while the starboard tab's actuator was placed on the elevator undersurface. (Lou Drendel)

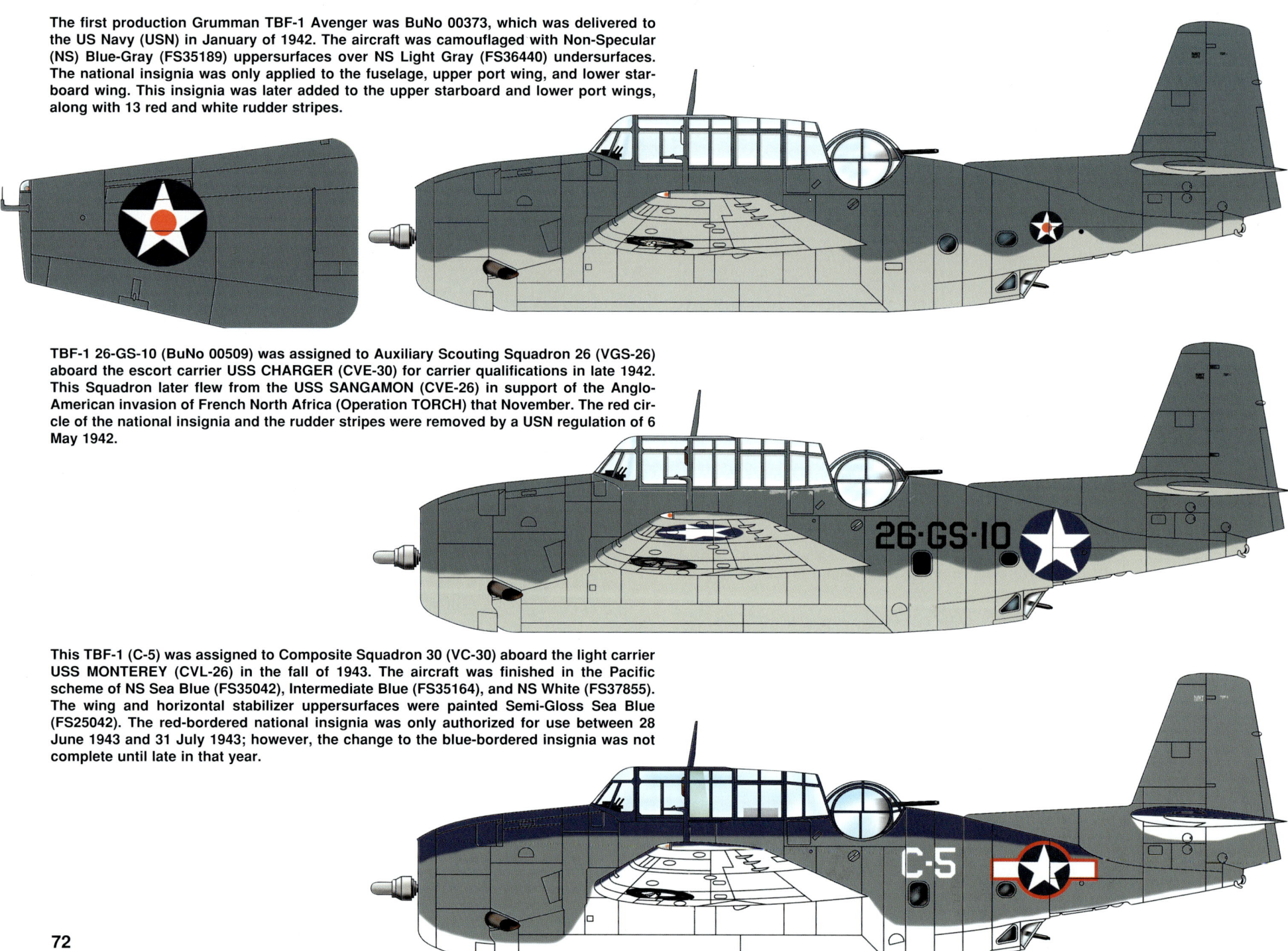

The first production Grumman TBF-1 Avenger was BuNo 00373, which was delivered to the US Navy (USN) in January of 1942. The aircraft was camouflaged with Non-Specular (NS) Blue-Gray (FS35189) uppersurfaces over NS Light Gray (FS36440) undersurfaces. The national insignia was only applied to the fuselage, upper port wing, and lower starboard wing. This insignia was later added to the upper starboard and lower port wings, along with 13 red and white rudder stripes.

TBF-1 26-GS-10 (BuNo 00509) was assigned to Auxiliary Scouting Squadron 26 (VGS-26) aboard the escort carrier USS CHARGER (CVE-30) for carrier qualifications in late 1942. This Squadron later flew from the USS SANGAMON (CVE-26) in support of the Anglo-American invasion of French North Africa (Operation TORCH) that November. The red circle of the national insignia and the rudder stripes were removed by a USN regulation of 6 May 1942.

This TBF-1 (C-5) was assigned to Composite Squadron 30 (VC-30) aboard the light carrier USS MONTEREY (CVL-26) in the fall of 1943. The aircraft was finished in the Pacific scheme of NS Sea Blue (FS35042), Intermediate Blue (FS35164), and NS White (FS37855). The wing and horizontal stabilizer uppersurfaces were painted Semi-Gloss Sea Blue (FS25042). The red-bordered national insignia was only authorized for use between 28 June 1943 and 31 July 1943; however, the change to the blue-bordered insignia was not complete until late in that year.

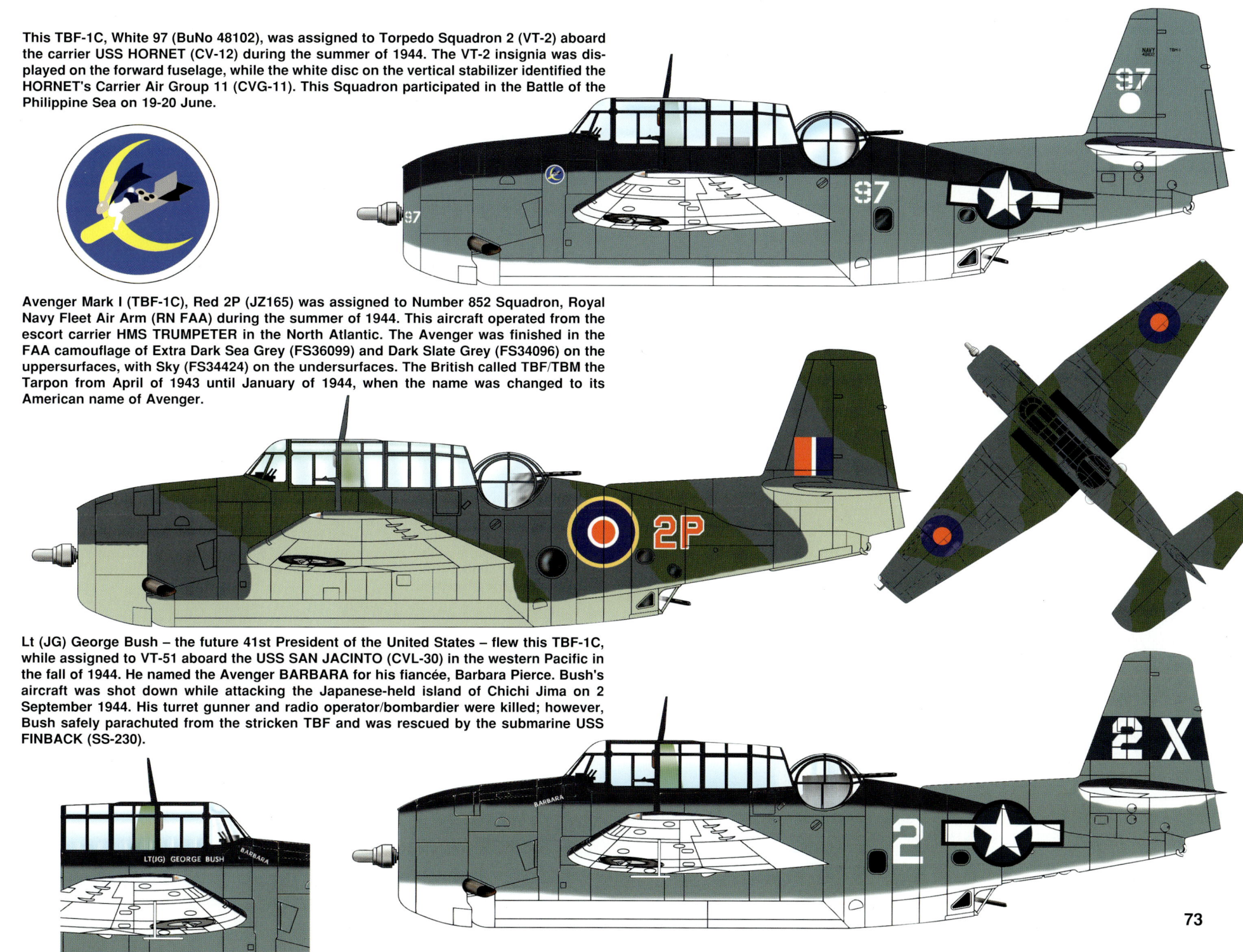

This TBF-1C, White 97 (BuNo 48102), was assigned to Torpedo Squadron 2 (VT-2) aboard the carrier USS HORNET (CV-12) during the summer of 1944. The VT-2 insignia was displayed on the forward fuselage, while the white disc on the vertical stabilizer identified the HORNET's Carrier Air Group 11 (CVG-11). This Squadron participated in the Battle of the Philippine Sea on 19-20 June.

Avenger Mark I (TBF-1C), Red 2P (JZ165) was assigned to Number 852 Squadron, Royal Navy Fleet Air Arm (RN FAA) during the summer of 1944. This aircraft operated from the escort carrier HMS TRUMPETER in the North Atlantic. The Avenger was finished in the FAA camouflage of Extra Dark Sea Grey (FS36099) and Dark Slate Grey (FS34096) on the uppersurfaces, with Sky (FS34424) on the undersurfaces. The British called TBF/TBM the Tarpon from April of 1943 until January of 1944, when the name was changed to its American name of Avenger.

Lt (JG) George Bush – the future 41st President of the United States – flew this TBF-1C, while assigned to VT-51 aboard the USS SAN JACINTO (CVL-30) in the western Pacific in the fall of 1944. He named the Avenger BARBARA for his fiancée, Barbara Pierce. Bush's aircraft was shot down while attacking the Japanese-held island of Chichi Jima on 2 September 1944. His turret gunner and radio operator/bombardier were killed; however, Bush safely parachuted from the stricken TBF and was rescued by the submarine USS FINBACK (SS-230).

TBF-1Cs of Marine Torpedo Bomber Squadron 242 (VMTB-242) taxi for take off on Bougainville on 17 February 1944. During World War II, 23 Marine squadrons operated Avengers on ground support and training missions. Marine Avenger units began operating from aircraft carriers in June of 1944; within a year, these Squadrons were part of nine Marine Carrier Air Groups (MCVGs). (USMC via Norman E. Taylor Collection)

Avenger TR Mark II (6C, JZ511) leads a vic (three-aircraft formation) of aircraft from a Royal Naval Air Station in Britain. JZ511 was one of 334 TBM-1Cs delivered for use by the Fleet Air Arm during World War II. A total of 958 Avengers were delivered to the United Kingdom under the Lend-Lease program. British Avengers had domes fitted in place of the aft fuselage window immediately aft of the wing and British radios were installed. (Norman E. Taylor Collection)

Five TBF-1s assigned to Auxiliary Scouting Squadron 29 (VGS-29) fly in stepped formation on a training mission during the latter half of 1942. These early Avengers lacked the wing-mounted .50 caliber (12.7MM) machine guns, which replaced the cowl-mounted .30 caliber (7.62MM) weapon fitted to the TBF-1. VGS-29 – renamed Composite Squadron 29 (VC-29) on 1 March 1943 – deployed aboard the USS SANTEE (CVE-29) in August of 1943. (US Navy via Warren Bodie)

A stepped echelon formation of five TBF-1s, led by F-T 48, fly a training mission in mid-1943. The Avengers were finished in the Blue-Gray over Light Gray camouflage scheme, with the short-lived national insignia with red trim. US personnel in the Pacific felt the red trim could be mistaken in a flash for the Japanese red *Hinomaru* (rising sun) emblem. TBF/TBM pilots often flew their aircraft with their canopies open, exposing themselves to the breeze. (US Navy via Norman E. Taylor)

TBM-3, White 113, flies past medium altitude clouds while on a mission. The TBM-3 was the most heavily produced Avenger model, with 4664 examples produced from the spring of 1944 until the summer of 1945. This model featured the more powerful 1900 HP R-2600-20 engine, Mark 5 zero length rocket launchers, and improved cockpit lighting. The Eastern Aircraft Division of General Motors built all TBMs at their five plants in New Jersey, New York, and Maryland. (Norman E. Taylor Collection.)

White 1, a TBM-3 of Marine Air Group 24 (MAG-24), was used for daily mail flights between Marine garrisons in Peiping (now Beijing) and Tientsin (now Tianjin), China. It was preparing to takeoff from Nan Yuan Field in Peiping in late 1945. A Marine sergeant (second from left) was conversing with a Chinese officer visiting the airfield. The Avenger's large bomb bay made the aircraft useful in the utility transport role after World War II. (Norman E. Taylor Collection)

A well-worn and unarmed TBM-3 sits on a ramp in April of 1944. The aircraft was finished in overall Glossy Sea Blue (FS15042) with the national insignia in Glossy Insignia Blue (FS15044) and Glossy Insignia White (FS17855). The Insignia Blue insignia disc and outline were soon deleted and the white directly painted onto the Glossy Sea Blue finish. This style of US national insignia was formalized in a Navy circular dated 10 June 1946. (Norman E. Taylor Collection)

Eastern Aircraft TBM-1C, Black 2, was assigned to Composite Squadron 12 (VC-12) aboard the USS CHARGER (CVE-30) in the North Atlantic during the fall of 1944. The Avenger was camouflaged in the Atlantic Anti-Submarine Scheme II, which consisted of Dark Gull Gray (FS36231) uppersurfaces with Non-Specular White (FS37855) sides and undersurfaces. This superceded the Atlantic Anti-Submarine Scheme I of Dark Gull Gray, Light Gull Gray (FS36440), and White.

White 110 was a TBM-3 assigned to VT-82 aboard the USS BENNINGTON (CV-20) in February of 1945. The aircraft was overall Glossy Sea Blue (FS15042) with Glossy Insignia Blue (FS15044) and Glossy Insignia White (FS17855) national markings. The white arrowhead on the rudder and the upper starboard and lower port ailerons was the BENNINGTON's air group insignia. In early 1945, VT-82's Avengers attacked enemy targets in the Japanese home islands.

White X/376 was an Avenger Mark I (JZ114) assigned to Number 848 Squadron aboard the British aircraft carrier HMS FORMIDABLE in August of 1945. This Squadron's aircraft attacked Japanese targets on Okinawa, Formosa (Taiwan), and the Japanese home islands in the last summer of World War II. Aircraft assigned to the British Pacific Fleet wore Blue and White roundels with bars on the fuselage, upper port wing, and lower starboard wing. These markings prevented US forces from confusing the British aircraft for the Japanese.

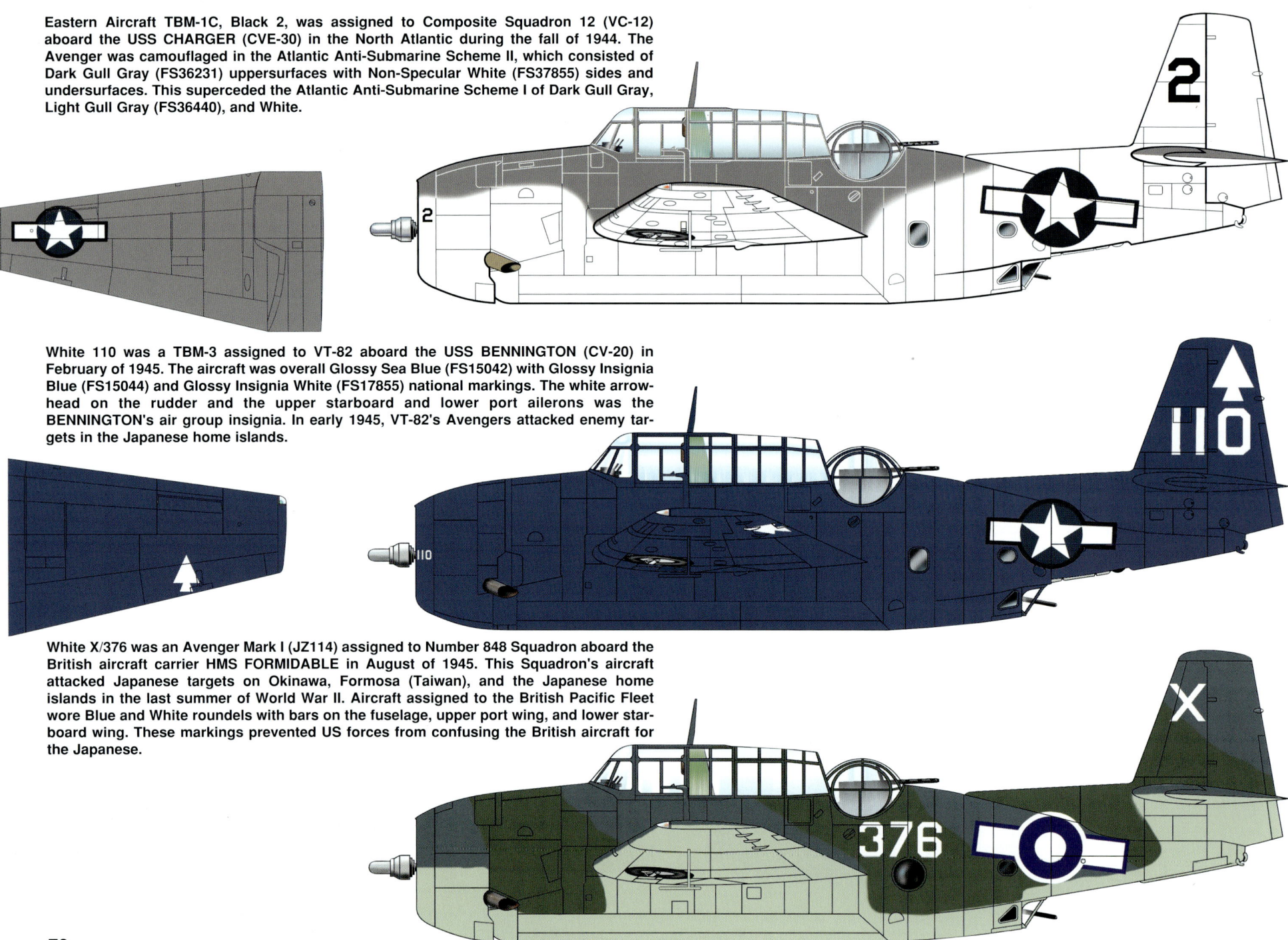

This TBM-3U (UD-35, BuNo 69329) was used for target towing and liaison duties with Utility Squadron 4 (VU-4) at Naval Air Station (NAS) Norfolk, Virginia in 1948. The fuselage was Glossy Sea Blue, while the wings, horizontal stabilizers, elevators, and vertical stabilizers were Glossy Orange Yellow (FS13538). The rudder and wing bands were Glossy Insignia Red (FS11136). All armament was removed and the canopy elongated on the TBM-3U, which served with seven USN utility squadrons in the post-World War II period.

This TBM-3S (Y-AR, 53682) was assigned to Number 880 Squadron (later VS-880), Royal Canadian Navy (RCN) at RCN Air Station Shearwater, Nova Scotia in 1952. The aircraft – locally designated the Avenger AS Mark 3 – was used for anti-submarine patrols off Canada's Atlantic coast between 1950 and 1957. This Avenger retained the USN finish of overall Glossy Sea Blue.

France's *Aéronautique Navale* (*Aéronavale*; Naval Aviation) operated the TBM-3W in the anti-submarine 'hunter' role alongside TBM-3S 'killer' aircraft. This Glossy Sea Blue Avenger was assigned to *Flottille* (First-Line Squadron) 4F aboard the French aircraft carrier ARROMANCHES during the fall of 1956. The black and yellow wing and fuselage stripes indicated the aircraft's deployment during the Anglo-French Suez conflict against Egypt that November.

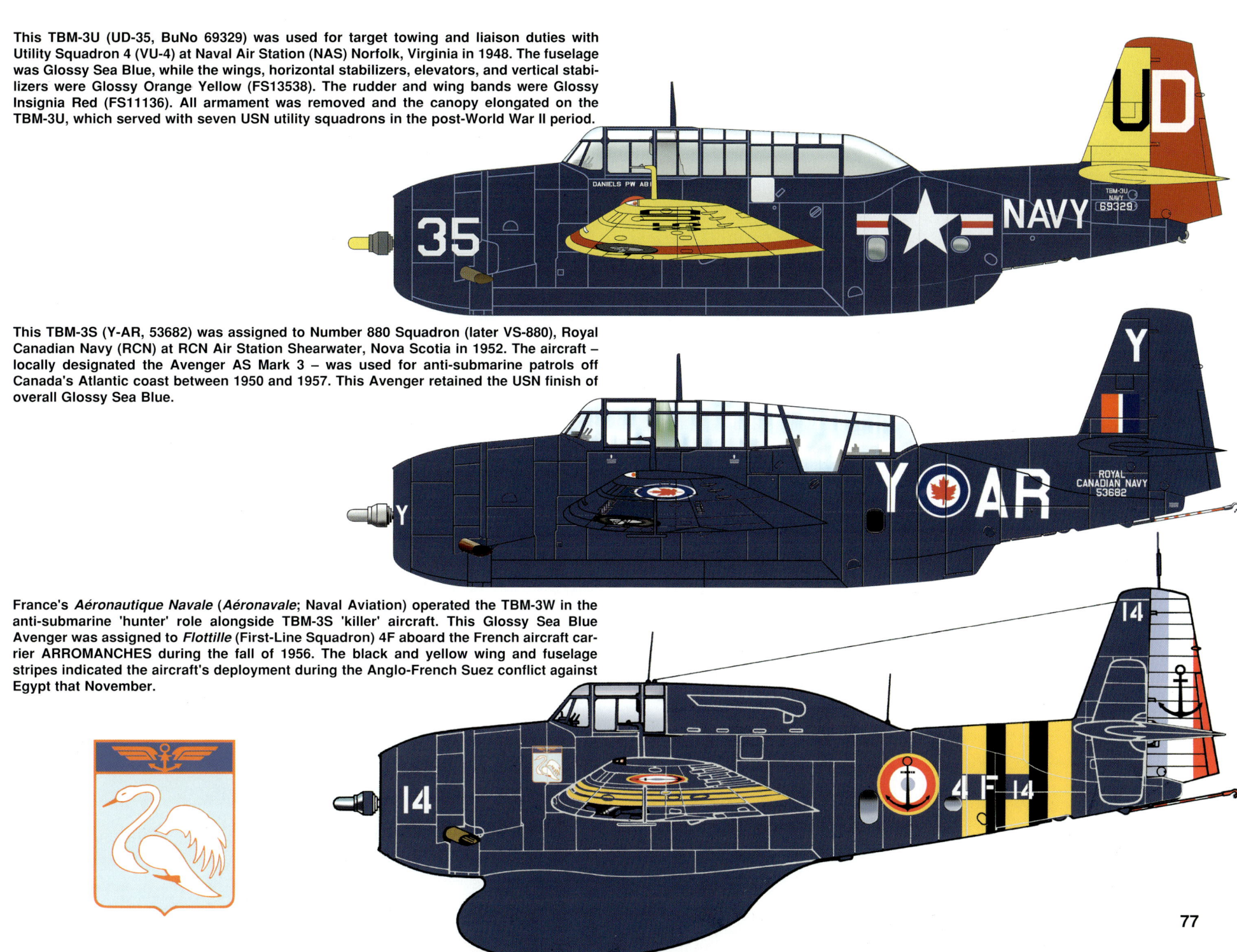

Five Avengers fly over the COMMENCEMENT BAY class escort carrier USS SAIDOR (CVE-117) in September of 1946. Escort carriers did not operate with the fast carrier task forces, but were primarily employed as convoy escorts. Composite Squadrons (VCs) of TBMs and F4Fs/FM Wildcat Fighters embarked on the CVEs were equipped for Anti-Submarine Warfare (ASW). The VCs generally consisted of nine Wildcats and 12 Avengers, although these totals varied among escort carriers. (USMC via Norman E. Taylor collection.)

Two TBM-3Es – BuNo 91704 on the port side – fly in formation during the late 1940s. The red center bars were added to the US national insignia on 14 January 1947. In 1946, the US Navy combined Torpedo (VT) and Dive Bomber (VB) squadrons into Attack Squadrons (VA). The Avenger was the first aircraft assigned to these units and served in the Attack role until the introduction of the Douglas AD Skyraider in the late 1940s. (Norman E. Taylor collection)

A TBM-3S (SA-301) was displayed at the Cleveland National Air Races in August of 1947. The -3S version was a TBM-3E modified for the ASW 'killer' mission. A radar operator rode in the aft cockpit space formerly occupied by the turret gunner. Mark 5 rocket launchers were retained under the wings; however, all machine guns were removed from the TBM-3S. (Warren Bodie via Norman E. Taylor collection)

This TBM-3W2 (BuNo 91454) was parked at Love Field, Dallas, Texas on 5 August 1954. The Avenger was assigned to a Naval Reserve unit at NAS (Naval Air Station) Willow Grove, Pennsylvania, as indicated by the International Orange (FS12197) aft fuselage band. The undersurface radome housed the AN/APS-20 radar antenna. This radar was optimized for detecting submarine snorkels and had an effective range of 135 nautical miles (250.2 км). (Norman E. Taylor collection.)

This TBM-3S (AR-Y, 53682) was assigned to No. 880 Squadron of the Royal Canadian Navy (RCN). The pod under the starboard wing housed an AN/APS-4 search radar, which supported the aircraft's role as a 'killer' in anti-submarine 'hunter-killer' teams with TBM-3Ws. Canada received 125 Avengers from the US Navy in 1950-52, which were designated Avenger AS Mark 3s by the RCN. They remained in front line Canadian service until 1957. (Warren Bodie)

This overall Glossy Sea Blue TBM-3S (53678) was assigned to *Escadrille* (Second-Line Squadron) 3S of the French *Aéronautique Navale* at Cuers, France in 1965. The Squadron's insignia appeared on the forward fuselage, ahead of the canopy area. France acquired 140 Avengers from the US under the MDAP between 1951 and 1958. These aircraft operated in the anti-submarine role from the French carriers ARROMANCHES, BOIS BELLEAU, and LAFAYETTE. (Norman E. Taylor collection)

White 266 (XB328) was an Avenger Mk 4 (TBM-3E) assigned to ASW duties with the Royal Navy. This is one of 100 Avengers delivered to Britain in 1953, under the US Mutual Defense Assistance Program (MDAP). The British flew the Avengers on ASW work until 1955 – when they were replaced by Fairey Gannets – and on second-line duties until 1962. This overall Glossy Sea Blue Avenger displayed the HEP CAT nose art on the engine cowling. (Norman E. Taylor Collection)

This TBM-3E (NL7001C/85794) is owned by Coke Stuart and was marked as the TBM-1C flown by President George Bush in World War II. This aircraft was parked at Titusville, Florida on 9 March 1991. After their military service, several Avengers were used as fire bombers over North American forests. Over 100 TBFs/TBMs survive in the world today, including several in flying condition in the US and several other countries. (Norman E. Taylor)

Carrier Aircraft and Carriers

1036 F6F Hellcat in Action

1064 SBD Dauntless in Action

1145 F4U Corsair in Action

4005 US Aircraft Carriers in Action, Part 1

4009 Escort Carriers in Action

4010 Essex Class Carriers in Action

from squadron/signal publications